1–2 PETER

AND

JUDE

WESLEY BIBLE STUDIES

wphonline.com

CONTENTS

INTRODUCTION

Life Transformation

Peter is one of the most interesting and influential figures in the New Testament and in the formation of the early church. A born leader, gregarious, tenacious, and bold, his name is often mentioned first in lists of the apostles. Once the early Christians began to grow in number, Peter assumed the prime position of leadership given to him by Christ himself. Yet Peter did not behave in this position of power with the audacity and self-confidence that a younger Peter might have. Instead, he exercised his authority with zealous humility. Peter was at once intense, charismatic, and modest, always directing attention to Jesus.

During this study, you will examine the two surviving letters from Peter. Here the once-boisterous apostle exhibits a matured faith by reinforcing Christ's call to personal holiness, embracing suffering, and exuding personal humility.

A third letter under study, the epistle from Jude, packs a powerful punch. Though brief, this letter contains one of the starkest warnings in all of Scripture. If the church can be described as a body, then Jude warns of a virus that will, if not detected and eradicated, wreak havoc on the church. This letter, combined with Peter's two, provides a wealth of practical teaching that will yield three insights in this study.

HOLINESS IS AN EVERYDAY MATTER

Like many modern-day followers of Jesus, Peter may have wished he could forget the youthful indiscretions that characterized his early days in the faith. His missteps as a companion of Christ are well-documented in the Gospels. And during his early days as a leader, Peter struggled to reconcile the freedom we have in Christ with the strict demands of the Old Testament Scriptures. So it comes as no surprise that a major theme of Peter's later teaching is the importance of the choices we make in daily behavior. While holiness is a matter of the heart, Peter rightly emphasizes that our love for God will be played out in the things we choose to do each day. We can talk about holiness—and should—but in the concrete world in which we live, holiness is action. This is not legalism. Holiness does not consist in keeping a list of rules but is the inevitable result of having a pure heart—living a changed life.

SUFFERING STRENGTHENS THE BODY

The inevitability of suffering is a second major theme in Peter's writing. Christians will suffer on behalf of Christ. Peter's aim is to affirm that truth and to encourage those who are currently suffering persecution for the sake of Jesus. This sharing in Christ's suffering, he said, only makes the body stronger. We see this truth borne out today as the church is growing explosively in some areas where Christians are now being persecuted. We see it in other, more subtle, ways in our own culture as godly living is mocked and sacred things are defamed. Any challenge to faith will strengthen the faithful.

The writings of Peter—along with Paul and James—call us not only to endure suffering, but also to delight in it. When we are persecuted, we have the honor of sharing in the afflictions of our Lord.

WE ARE A BODY

From Jude we learn another truth about the body of Christ, a lesson of health management. Jude warned early Christians of false teachers in their midst and made the amazing claim that each of us is responsible for the health of the community. When the church faces any problem, it is easiest to believe that others are responsible, that someone else can or should do something about it. Not so, according to Jude. We dare not wait for others to confront error and correct the church. We are all responsible for the health of this body.

As you study these candid, practical letters, you'll gain a sense of solidarity with the millions of Christians who have come before you—and the many who will follow. From Pontus to Peoria, from Cleveland to Cappadocia, we each bear the name of the Lord Jesus Christ.

FULL SALVATION

1 Peter 1:1–12

Salvation begins with the new birth and continues
through glorification in heaven.

When a family-owned business fails, it is usually in the third
generation. The first generation works hard to establish the business,
working long hours and making financial sacrifices to get the
enterprise started. The next generation, sons and daughters of the
founders, remember those sacrifices. Although they were only
children at the time, they recall their parents working late into
the night and feeling anxiety about paying bills. The second
generation witnessed the struggle and so values its fruit. The
third generation, however, may lack this perspective. These
grandchildren of the founders cannot recall a time when there
was no business or when it was not successful. They were born to
prosperity and, as a result, may esteem it too lightly. It is this
generation's greed or mishandling that may cause the business
to fail.

Peter was writing to "third generation" Christians, as it were.
Realizing that this group of believers had not yet seen the tests
of faith that were sure to come, Peter's motive was to inspire
them to value their salvation and to guard it zealously. This study
challenges us to realize how precious is the salvation that Jesus
bought for us with His own blood, and to prepare ourselves for
the day when we will meet Him face-to-face.

COMMENTARY

First Peter falls, along with 2 Peter and Jude, in the group of letters known as the General Epistles because the addressees are less specifically or clearly identified than in the other Epistles (note the exception of 3 John). The context of the day was persecution and separation. His recipients were "strangers in the world, scattered throughout Pontus, Galatia, Cappadocia, Asia and Bithynia" (1 Pet. 1:1). From our perspective, they were not scattered widely, since all those named locations are found in present-day Turkey. But even a twenty-mule train or a mile on a camel took a while in A.D. 63. By that date, the Christian communities were a mix of Gentile and Jewish believers with the majority becoming Gentile in character.

Kingdom Communiqué (1 Pet. 1:1–2)

Peter began with personal identification of the kingdom kind. His return address is not only Peter, but **Peter, an apostle of Jesus Christ** (v. 1). Wouldn't his recipients have known about his apostleship? Wouldn't those who delivered the letter have assured the faithful it was really from him? So his reason involved emphasizing truth. His identification as **an apostle of Jesus Christ** announced, "This is kingdom business, important information contained herein." It underscored his authority, yet as one whose mission (an apostle, "a sent one") and authority were both derived from the Savior and Messiah whom they all served. The epistle is addressed: **To God's elect, strangers in the world, scattered throughout Pontus, Galatia, Cappadocia, Asia and Bithynia** (v. 1). Interestingly, both the translators of the NIV and KJV attempted clarification rather than translation. The Greek order is "to elect strangers scattered throughout" the various areas. The KJV has "to the strangers scattered throughout" and removes "elect" from verse 1 and places it with "God" in verse 2. The NIV brought **God** into verse 1 and added the phrase

in the world. The theology is correct in both instances: God does the electing. But both miss the intent of Peter referring to Christians as "elect strangers scattered." Leaving the Greek intact has their election, stranger status, and scattering as *all* happening according to the foreknowledge of God. God is not surprised by our status in life, we are strategically placed by His intelligent plan! So not only are we **chosen according to the foreknowledge of God the Father** (v. 2), but we are "chosen strangers scattered" **according to the foreknowledge of God the Father!** The tenor of the passage points to something more than simple awareness. It is active planning and strategic manipulation of His people in pursuit of the goal that all nations receive His Son.

[handwritten margin notes: "All 3"; "God's Intent + purpose for each of us"]

WORDS FROM WESLEY

1 Peter 1:2

According to the foreknowledge of God—Speaking after the manner of men. Strictly speaking, there is no foreknowledge, no more than after-knowledge, with God: but all things are known to Him as present, from eternity to eternity. This is therefore no other than an instance of the divine condescension to our low capacities. *Elect*—By the free love and almighty power of God, taken out of, separated from, the world. Election, in the Scripture sense, is God's doing any thing that our merit or power have no part in. The true predestination, or fore-appoinment of God is, 1. He that believeth shall be saved, from the guilt and power of sin. 2. He that endureth to the end, shall be saved eternally. They who receive the precious gift of faith, thereby become the sons of God: and being sons, they shall receive the Spirit of holiness, to walk as Christ also walked. Throughout every part of this appointment of God, promise and duty go hand in hand. All is free gift; and yet such is the gift, that the final issue depends on our future obedience to the heavenly call. (ENNT)

So our choosing and placement have not only been accomplished conforming to the Father's thoughtfulness, but also **through the sanctifying work of the Spirit** (v. 2). Character is involved!

How we live where we live is vital. God's plan requires our sanctification, so He engineers its accomplishment in the midst of living! We are not only sanctified *for* service, we are also sanctified *in* service. So we have the plan and instrument, now the purpose: **for obedience to Jesus Christ and sprinkling by his blood** (v. 2). The Greek word order again yields significance: literally "for obedience and sprinkling by the blood of Jesus Christ." This connects **obedience** and **sprinkling** with the purpose, suggesting more unity than the NIV rendering. The KJV stands more true at this point. Obedience in the context of persecution recalls the crucifixion of Jesus Christ and reminds of the privilege and blessing received when persecuted for righteousness' sake (Matt. 5:10–12). Perhaps it also hints that persecutions they endured were only a "sprinkling" of the cross; they had not yet known the extent of the Messiah's sufferings. About two years after writing this, Peter chose to be crucified upside down so as not to receive the honor of a death so like the Savior's—a powerful point of motivation for those examining his words after hearing the manner of his death.

●

WORDS FROM WESLEY

1 Peter 1:3

A second scriptural mark of those who are born of God, is hope. Thus St. Peter, speaking to all the children of God who were then scattered abroad, saith, "Blessed be the God and Father of our Lord Jesus Christ, which, according to his abundant mercy, hath begotten us again unto a lively hope" (1 Pet. 1:3). . . . A *lively* or *living* hope, saith the apostle; because there is also a *dead* hope, as well as a dead faith; a hope which is not from God, but from the enemy of God and man—as evidently appears by its fruits; for, as it is the offspring of pride, so it is the parent of every evil word and work; whereas, every man that hath in him this living hope, is "holy as He that calleth him is holy": Every man that can truly say to his brethren in Christ, "Beloved, now are we the sons of God, and we shall see him as he is," "purifieth himself, even as He is pure." (WJW, vol. 5, 216)

Only as these elect continued in relationship to the Godhead in plan, instrument, and purpose could they expect the fulfillment of Peter's completed greeting: **Grace and peace be yours in abundance** (1 Pet. 1:2). It is common practice to rip off greetings in conversation without reflecting on meaning, yet even for us, written greetings reflect more thought. In the carefully worded construction before us, Peter not only meant it, he increased its likelihood.

Rejoicing Reminder (1 Pet. 1:3–9)

Praise be to the God and Father of our Lord Jesus Christ! (v. 3). In verse 3, Peter exploded in anticipatory praise: the thoughts encapsulated in the previous verses were to be given fuller expression. What a wonderful God! He put this all together! And look: **In his great mercy he has given us new birth into a living hope through the resurrection of Jesus Christ from the dead** (v. 3). Some might have objected to the thought that God actually intended for their persecution. It certainly is not God's pristine will that any should suffer, nor even that His Son should have died on the cross, but God would not have had to send His Son if the world had been pristine. Not only did Christ die while we were yet sinners (Rom. 5:8), but we also are to die while *they* are yet sinners. Remember, Christian, it was out of **his great mercy** that **he** gave **us new birth** (1 Pet. 1:3). That new birth was not just a second chance, but an entrance into a radically different life. Never before had those newly born been the possessors of **a living hope**. Nor could the guarantee be any more powerfully demonstrated than in **the resurrection of Jesus Christ from the dead**. Our new creation is not only **a living hope**, but also **an inheritance that can never perish, spoil or fade—kept in heaven for you** (v. 4). God granted an entrance into the reality of spiritual life, freeing us from the momentary even as we live in the moment. Freedom because we have a vitality that death cannot diminish and a possession preserved from perishing!

(Verse 5) turns this wonder toward these Christians. They are ones **who through faith are shielded by God's power**. Yes, while it's so bad, God is protecting. Ask yourself, "Am I stronger than my enemies?" In Pontus, numbers were not in the favor of the Christian community. In the physical world, Christians are often at a distinct disadvantage. So explain survival *and* expansion: **through faith** you **are shielded by God's power**. In God even if we die, we win, because we **are shielded . . . until the coming of the salvation that is ready to be revealed in the last time** (v. 5). That salvation, though, was not what a martyr ascended to upon death. The martyr would have tasted more than the earthbound, but full disclosure waits even for the dead. A greater lack of knowledge exists for the unrepentant persecutor. Those unfaithful identified in every knee will bow and every tongue confess (Isa. 45:23; Rom. 14:11; Phil. 2:10–11) will see the salvation, but not enjoy it. Until that time we **are shielded by God's power**; at that time we will be revealed in God's power (1 Pet. 1:5)!

WORDS FROM WESLEY

1 Peter 1:6

The persons spoken of here were *grieved*: The heaviness they were in was neither more nor less than *sorrow*, or *grief*—a passion which every child of man is well acquainted with.

It is probable our translators rendered it *heaviness* (though a less common word), to denote two things: First, the degree, and next the continuance, of it. It does indeed seem, that it is not a slight or inconsiderable degree of grief which is here spoken of; but such as makes a strong impression upon, and sinks deep into, the soul. Neither does this appear to be a transient sorrow, such as passes away in an hour; but rather, such as, having taken fast hold of the heart, is not presently shaken off, but continues for some time, as a settled temper, rather than a passion, even in them that have living faith in Christ, and the genuine love of God in their hearts. (WJW, vol. 6, 94)

Can't you hear yourself reply to Peter's statement: **In this you greatly rejoice** (v. 6) with, "We do? Oh, that's right. I forgot. We do!" This epistle is a reminder of basic truths in Scripture and, therefore, basic truths of Christian living. **Though now for a little while** (v. 6) encompasses a variety of possibilities. What now attends your life that is less than heavenly? Some things a bit less: the pleasures of church, home, family, and friends; some far less: crime, pornography, persecution, and death. These elect strangers **may have had to suffer grief in all kinds of trials** (v. 6). Many things should not be, but we waste energy lamenting them. Rather, see them in another light. A light that shines through the greater truth: God in our circumstance. Another cause for rejoicing is that **these** trials **have come so that your faith . . . may be proved genuine** (v. 7). The Greek brings to mind a foundry where metal is tested to ascertain its quality and fired to improve it. Christian faith, treated likewise by God, is compared favorably to gold: **faith—of greater worth than gold, which perishes even though refined by fire** (v. 7). Not only is faith more valuable, gold and its value won't last. Tested faith will serve an eternally valuable purpose: **praise, glory and honor when Jesus Christ is revealed** (v. 7). Yes, **praise, glory and honor** *to* Jesus, and revealing of **praise, glory and honor** conferred *by* Jesus upon the faithful. The witnesses will be the very ones who were persecutors.

But the end-times revealing party is not just an unveiling to the rest of the world. Christians get to see Jesus in His fullness as well: **Though you have not seen him . . . and even though you do not see him now** (v. 8). Peter drew this reality as a commendation of their spiritual maturity and a reminder of a needed focus. He remembered when Jesus, who as "an apostle of Jesus Christ" (v. 1) he *has* seen and heard, said to Thomas, "Because you have seen me, you have believed; blessed are those who have not seen and yet have believed" (John 20:29). So there is a blessedness now because **you love him** and **believe in him** (1 Pet. 1:8). A special blessedness because Jesus holds a unique place in His heart for those who have loved Him without benefit of human contact. It is a reflection of our own time-bound need for the physical, but we can hardly read the next phrase without hearing it as a reminder: **you . . . are filled with an inexpressible and glorious joy** (v. 8). Yes, now that you point me away from the moment to my purpose for living, there is an unspeakably wondrous joy that overwhelms! And that joy reflects the present, progressive attainment of faith's **goal . . . the salvation of your souls** (v. 9).

WORDS FROM WESLEY
1 Peter 1:7

The first and great end of God's permitting the temptations which bring heaviness on His children, is the trial of their faith, which is tried by these, even as gold by the fire. Now we know, gold tried in the fire is purified thereby; is separated from its dross. And so is faith in the fire of temptation; the more it is tried, the more it is purified—yea, and not only purified, but also strengthened, confirmed, increased abundantly, by so many more proofs of the wisdom and power, the love and faithfulness, of God. This, then—to increase our faith—is one gracious end of God's permitting those manifold temptations.

They serve to try, to purify, to confirm, and increase that living hope also, whereunto "the God and Father of our Lord Jesus Christ hath begotten us again of his abundant mercy." Indeed our hope cannot but increase, in the same proportion with our faith. On this foundation it stands: Believing in His name, living by faith in the Son of God, we hope for, we have a confident expectation of, the glory which shall be revealed; and, consequently, whatever strengthens our faith, increases our hope also. At the same time it increases our joy in the Lord, which cannot but attend a hope full of immortality. (WJW, vol. 6, 99–100)

Prophetic Providence (1 Pet. 1:10–12)

What a great thing **this salvation** (v. 10) is! Your heroes, **the prophets** (v. 10) and **even** the **angels** (v. 12) envy you. What a tremendous truth encased in few verses. Peter exposed the workings of inspiration more fully here than perhaps is done anywhere else. Disclosure came to strengthen the resolve of Christians living under persecution. Not only did God have a strategic purpose in your placement, He has been active on your behalf a very long time. **Concerning this salvation, the prophets, who spoke of the grace that was to come to you** (v. 10); they spoke of what they were told. And they **searched intently and with the greatest care** (v. 10) because they knew these words formed a momentous truth. Just think: Amos heard from God; Amos spoke; it was written; and then Amos spent the next forty years studying what was said. These prophets were workmen "who [did] not need to be ashamed and who correctly handle[d] the word of truth" (2 Tim. 2:15). It was precious in their hands. They were eager to know when the Messiah would come and suffer and when triumph would come. They were **trying to find out the time and circumstances to which the Spirit of Christ in them was pointing when he predicted the sufferings of Christ and the glories that would follow** (1 Pet. 1:11). Peter's present knowledge reflected back on their contemplation. How much did the prophets know about what they said? Less than they desired: **It was revealed to them that they were not serving themselves but you** (v. 12). God had them speak and write for the benefit of elect strangers scattered, including you! And the same God still operates. For the things they prophesied **have now been told you by those who have preached the gospel to you by the Holy Spirit sent from heaven** (v. 12). These prophesies are now active through the wondrous workings of God the Father, the Son, and the Holy Spirit. So marvelous and heavenly are they that **even angels long to look into these things** (v. 12).

DISCUSSION

Peter wrote this letter to prepare the church for the persecution they were likely to face in the near future. He wanted to strengthen them and give them hope.

1. Peter wrote his letter during a time of great persecution and wanted to be sure his readers were ready to meet God. What requirements did he list for them?

2. How is each of the three requirements listed in 1 Peter 1:1–2 represented by a member of the Trinity?

3. What did Peter mean by "foreknowledge"? Do you think this implies that we do not have a choice about our own salvation?

4. What do you think Peter meant by "the sanctifying work of the Spirit"?

5. How does "obedience to Jesus Christ" and "sprinkling of his blood" incorporate the truth that "faith without works is dead"?

6. Peter seemed especially grateful for Christ's "great mercy." Based on what you know of Peter's life, why would that be true? In what ways is the same true for you?

7. Which statements in Peter's message do you think would give the most hope to people who were being persecuted?

8. Peter wrote about an inheritance that can never perish, spoil, or fade. What was he talking about?

9. How is it possible to have joy in spite of being persecuted for the faith? Do you sense a spirit of joy in your church? Do you feel that kind of joy?

10. How do trials refine faith? How have the things you've suffered strengthened your faith?

PRAYER

Most merciful God and Father, thank You for giving us a living hope in the resurrection of Your Son, our Lord. Help us not to squander this new birth, this second chance at life, but to live as those who have been brought back from the dead.

2

JOURNEY INTO HOLINESS

1 Peter 1:13—2:3

Salvation goes beyond forgiveness for sins to
produce a change in our very nature.

Have you been born again? That's a familiar question to
many Christians. Based on Jesus' teaching to Nicodemus (see
John 3:3), we realize that coming to Jesus initiates a dramatic life
change. "Yes!" many of us would enthusiastically respond to the
question. Many could even name a date, time, and place where
that occurred.

Yet salvation encompasses much more than a single moment in
our spiritual history. Salvation is both a present reality and a future
goal. Perhaps the question would be more accurate if asked, "Are
you now being saved?" Our salvation is a crisis and process, bringing
us to the goal of holiness—loving God with our whole heart.

Peter's writing explains the comprehensive nature of salvation.
Legally, it releases us from the guilt of sin, justifying us from our
past behaviors and attitudes. But salvation also corrects our moral
standing by regeneration, changing our character and essence.
Thus, God's salvation not only declares us righteous, but also
enables us to become righteous.

This study helps us comprehend the expansive goal of God's
work in our lives and urges us to keep going toward the goal of
complete salvation.

COMMENTARY

The recipients of this letter were clearly believers ("God's
elect," 1 Pet. 1:1), but equally clearly were not an accepted part

of their society. They are described as being "strangers" (1:1, 17; 2:11), "scattered" (1:1), and "aliens" (2:11). Note, too, that Peter addressed the believers as a group, the new Israel, God's chosen people, rather than as individuals. "Once you were not a people, but now you are the people of God" (2:10). He was writing a general letter to the church, not to individuals, and the theology contained here is the theology of the church. Perhaps that explains some of the similarities to Paul's letter to the Ephesians.

Already by 1:13, a number of the key themes of Peter's speaking and writing have emerged. In addition to the believers as the new Israel, another theme is that of salvation. Peter presented salvation not as a completed act, but as something begun that will be consummated at the return of Christ (v. 5), something that is the goal of faith (v. 9) that believers must "grow up in" (2:2). This sense of the coming consummation of salvation is part of what drives another theme, that of hope.

Because of Christ's death and resurrection, when we are born again (1:3), we are born into a living hope. This hope is living because it is founded on a living Savior! We are also born into an inheritance that is imperishable (v. 4). The future is bright for God's chosen ones! (See also 1:21; 3:5, 15.)

Yet one final theme revealed in the earliest verses of 1 Peter likely provides the key to the occasion for its writing. While the future is bright, the present is filled with trials and suffering (1:6–7). Believers must not lose hope. Christ also suffered, but glory would ultimately follow (v. 11). Peter warned that the believers should expect suffering (2:19; 4:12–13; 5:1, 9) but that sharing in Christ's sufferings brings glory to God and will ultimately result in sharing His glory (1:7; 4:13–14; 5:1, 4, 10). Clearly these young believers were facing suffering firsthand. Peter remembered only too clearly his own failure under threat of persecution (see John 18). As a spiritual father, he encouraged believers to persevere. The goal was the salvation of their souls (1 Pet. 9), and it would all be worth it when the glory was revealed (5:1).

With all of these themes introduced in the first twelve verses of chapter 1, verse 13 begins with focused instructions on the appropriate response of these new Christians.

Be Holy (1 Pet. 1:13–16)

Verse 13 starts with the word **therefore**, pointing back to what has been said in earlier verses. Peter instructed that in view of the new birth and its consequences and in view of the message of the prophets of old and of the preachers of the gospel, believers must do three things. They must prepare their minds for action, demonstrate self-control, and set their hope on the grace that comes through Christ.

The RSV translates the phrase **prepare your minds for action** (v. 13) with terminology that provides a vivid image. In the RSV, this phrase is translated "gird up your mind" and presents the image of a man of that time dressed in long, flowing robes. In order to be ready for action, he pulls up his long robe and tucks it in his belt, so that his legs are unencumbered and freedom of action is insured. Peter said this image should describe thinking Christians. Their minds should be free of encumbrances so they are clear-minded and sharp, ready for action.

In addition, Christians should be **self-controlled** or sober (v. 13). While the term may be applied to alcohol consumption, it has much broader application to all of life. Christians should be the masters of their habits and desires through the power of Christ. Willpower is critical! Later, in 4:7, Peter instructed, "Therefore be clear minded and self-controlled."

Peter also addressed the attitude: **set your hope fully on the grace to be given you when Jesus Christ is revealed** (1:13). The Christian's hope is found in nothing or no one else but Christ. Hope placed anywhere else will fail.

WORDS FROM WESLEY

1 Peter 1:15

The command of God, given by St. Peter, "Be ye holy, as he that hath called you is holy, in all manner of conversation," implies a promise that we shall be thus holy, if we are not wanting to ourselves. Nothing can be wanting on God's part: As He has called us to holiness, He is undoubtedly willing, as well as able, to work this holiness in us. For He cannot mock His helpless creatures, calling us to receive what He never intends to give. That He does call us thereto is undeniable; therefore He will give it if we are not disobedient to the heavenly calling. (WJW, vol. 5, 416)

Now a contrast becomes evident. Prior to their conversion, these believers were ignorant of God and consequently lived according to their **evil desires** (v. 14). As **obedient children** (or better, as children of obedience), their lives were to be characterized by different desires and a very different standard.

The heart of the standard for Christian living is the very character of God himself—and He is a **holy** God (v. 15). In the Old Testament, the term *holy* referred primarily to that which was distinct, separate, set apart, and entirely unlike any other. God is holy because He is so radically "other," separate from all uncleanness and defilement. In the Jewish Law, this command of verses 15 and 16 occurs four times: (1) Leviticus 11:44–45, in the context of instructions about clean and unclean foods; (2) Leviticus 19:2, about appropriate worship; (3) Leviticus 20:7, about personal choices and the punishment for sin; and (4) Leviticus 20:26, about instructions for a righteous nation. Holiness affects all of life and becomes the basis for our ethics as Christians. Later, Peter added clarity to this message when he indicated that believers actually "participate in the divine nature and escape the corruption in the world caused by evil desires" (2 Pet. 1:4).

Can believers live holy lives? The message of this letter and the rest of the New Testament is clear. Not only is it possible, it is absolutely necessary, for "without holiness no one will see the Lord" (Heb. 12:14). But if this is the case, what does it look like in practical terms? The rest of the passage begins to flesh out the answer for us.

Live as Strangers in Reverent Fear (1 Pet. 1:17–21)

Beginning with the rationale, Peter now set before these believers his next instruction. Knowing that God is a judge who judges impartially (that is, with justice—no favorites and no bullying!), **live your lives as strangers here in reverent fear** (v. 17).

Strangers are those who do not get overly attached to things. After all, they are not "at home." Peter built on this theme when he talked about the contrast between perishable and imperishable things. There is no point in building your life around things that perish. Even things like silver and gold are perishable and represent the purchase price of **the empty way of life** (v. 18) that came down through the heritage of these former unbelievers. (This indicates that there were Gentiles among the recipients. A Jewish heritage was not one of the **empty way of life**.)

In contrast to these empty and perishable things is the purchase price for the redemption of believers—**the precious blood of Christ, a lamb without blemish or defect** (v. 19). The **lamb** points to the Old Testament law concerning sacrifice. The sacrificial animal must be perfect, without any defect (Lev. 22:18–25), for God expects the very best. It also suggests the Passover lamb that provided for the deliverance of Israel from bondage. Because of Christ and His precious sacrifice, we believe in God and our **faith and hope are in** Him (1 Pet. 1:21). Note, too, that Christ's role was not a backup plan devised when God's original plan went awry. No, Christ **was chosen before the creation of the world** (v. 20) for this key role in the redemption of humanity!

In view of this tremendous sacrifice and imperishable gift, we must not live as though Christ's death and resurrection did not matter. Rather, the appropriate attitude is one of reverent fear. This is not fear as dread or panicked anxiety, but as reverential awe. An awesome price has been paid **for your sake** (v. 20). And it places upon us a serious responsibility we dare not take lightly!

Love One Another Deeply (1 Pet. 1:22–25)

Once again holiness of life becomes the foundation for Christian behavior. Peter indicated the believers had **purified** themselves **by obeying the truth** (v. 22). One of the aspects of holiness is that which is undefiled or pure. Paul described purity as a part of holiness when he placed impurity in contrast to holiness: "God did not call us to be impure, but to live a holy life" (1 Thess. 4:7). And what is it that purifies? **The truth** (1 Pet. 1:22). The truth comes **through the living and enduring word of God** (v. 23).

WORDS FROM WESLEY

1 Peter 1:23

If you have not already experienced this inward work of God, be your continual prayer: "Lord, add this to all thy blessings—let me be born again! Deny whatever thou pleasest, but deny not this; let me be 'born from above!' Take away whatsoever seemeth thee good—reputation, fortune, friends, health—only give me this, to be born of the Spirit, to be received among the children of God! Let me be born, 'not of corruptible seed, but incorruptible, by the word of God, which liveth and abideth for ever;' and then let me daily 'grow in grace, and in the knowledge of our Lord and Saviour Jesus Christ!' (WJW, vol. 6, 77)

As in the previous passage, the contrast between the temporal and the eternal becomes evident. Before they became Christians, the recipients of this letter were born of **perishable seed** (v. 23).

But having experienced the new birth, they are now born of **imperishable** seed. Peter went on to quote Isaiah 40:6–8 that describes the enduring nature of God's Word. The allusion here is probably to the parable of the sower in Luke 8:5–15, where the seed is the Word of God. To be born again is to be born of the Word of God, which is living and enduring. It is obedience to this Word that provides purity. The implication is unmistakable. Christians must be people of God's Word, learning and studying that they might be purified by this powerful Word.

If believers obey the Word and are purified by it, it seems inevitable that the fruit of such a life is love for others. That is the imperative verb found here. **Love one another deeply** (1 Pet. 1:22). This love is not a shallow, perishable thing that is natural to humans. Rather, it is something that springs out of a heart that has been purified by truth. Clearly God's Word changes our hearts (Heb. 4:12), and from a heart like God's, we are able to love others with His love.

WORDS FROM WESLEY
1 Peter 1:22

Having purified your souls by obeying the truth through the Spirit—Who bestows upon you freely, both obedience and purity of heart, and unfeigned love of the brethren; go on to still higher degrees of love: *love one another fervently*—With the most strong and tender affection, and yet *with a pure heart*—Pure from any spot of unholy desire, or inordinate passion. (ENNT)

Rid Yourselves of Evil and Crave What Is Good (1 Pet. 2:1–3)

In the final verses of this passage, Peter instructed these believers in a way that sounds very fatherly: He told them to **grow up** (v. 2). Maturity is the goal, and Peter was very practical about the way to achieve it. Maturity comes about as we rid ourselves of our old ways of life (**malice . . . deceit, hypocrisy, envy, and slander**, v. 1) and start craving the things of God.

But how do we get rid of these things? In many ways, Peter already provided the answer. "Prepare your minds for action; be self-controlled; set your hope fully on the grace" of Christ (1:13); live a holy life (1:15); give God the reverence He is due (1:17); purify yourself by "obeying the truth . . . love one another" (1:22). If we live in the positive ways the passage has directed, this negative instruction is not so difficult.

Because these believers were spiritual **babies** (2:2), it is "natural" (because believers have a new nature!) that they would **crave pure spiritual milk**. Peter said that, having tasted of God's goodness (see Ps. 34:8; Heb. 6:5), it will be natural for them to **crave** (that is, desire or long for) that which feeds and nourishes the Christian life (1 Pet. 2:2). And what is this **milk**? Generally speaking, it might be identified as the "things of God" and could include participation in worship, fellowship, and other aspects of the Christian life. But more particularly, the letter to the Hebrews (5:12–13) defines it as the "truths of God's word." Unlike the author of Hebrews, however, Peter did not separate spiritual nourishment into milk and solid food. Rather, he suggested only that believers should crave that which nourishes the spiritual life. The passage ends with a phrase that provides the motivation for all of the instruction in the passage: **the Lord is good** (1 Pet. 2:3)! Live your life in response to that goodness!

DISCUSSION

Peter reminded his readers that they are called to be holy as God is holy. The first step of faith is only the beginning of a transformational journey that will last a lifetime.

1. What do you think it means to "prepare your minds for action" (1 Pet. 1:13)?

2. List the places that you see Peter offering hope in this Scripture. What words of hope could you add, based on other Scriptures that come to mind?

3. Peter quoted God's command "Be holy, because I am holy" (v. 15)? What does it mean to be holy?

4. God judges each person's work impartially, according to Peter. By what standard will God judge?

5. What do you think Peter meant by "reverent fear" (v. 17)? To what degree do you see that reverent fear in today's church? What evidence supports your view?

6. What causes Peter's readers to have "faith and hope" (v. 21)?

7. Holiness is a cooperative effort between God and the believer. How do believers purify themselves? What is God's part in this?

8. How well is the church doing at eliminating the things mentioned in 2:1–2? How well are you doing?

9. What does it mean to "grow up" spiritually? What evidence would you expect to see in the life of a spiritually mature person?

PRAYER

Most gracious God, we thank You that You judge each person impartially. Help us mature in our faith that we may walk through this life in reverent fear, as strangers in a strange land, as pilgrims on a journey home.

BUILDING ON THE CORNERSTONE

1 Peter 2:4–12

We are called to live in a way that brings glory to God.

The foundation of a building is critical to its structural integrity. Without a strong foundation, there is inadequate support. If part of the foundation is removed, the building will begin to sag. Soon cracks will appear, and its integrity will be compromised. Structural strength must then be maintained throughout. Only by working together with Christ, the cornerstone of our faith, can we build a strong spiritual foundation. Though the foundation is strong, if the structure is flawed, disaster happens. When we, the church, build on the cornerstone, our foundation is sure.

While this might seem obvious when stated, Christians face the continual temptation to found their work on something other than Christ. We may resort to scientific principles, management theories, or good old-fashioned hard work as the better method for drawing people to the church and building them up in the faith. While each of these has its place, none is an adequate basis for making real spiritual change. Christ alone is the foundation of our faith.

This study issues a strong call to center our faith and practice on the only true foundation, Jesus Christ. While Paul referred to the church as a body, in which all the parts function under the direction of the head (see 1 Cor. 12:12–27), Peter's preferred analogy is a building. There is one cornerstone, and we each are living stones—each having its place in building God's kingdom.

COMMENTARY

As we read 1 Peter 2:4–12, our minds almost automatically return to an event in Peter's life some thirty years earlier. In Matthew 16:13–20, Peter had finally come to recognize Jesus as the Christ, the long-awaited Messiah. Jesus responded, "And I tell you that you are Peter, and on this rock I will build my church, and the gates of Hades will not overcome it" (Matt. 16:18). Of course, Peter's name (*Petros*) means "rock" and, since Jesus used the similar noun *petra* (also meaning "rock") in the same verse, many throughout history (especially within the Roman Catholic Church) have held that the church was built on the apostle Peter. As Protestants, however, we are convinced that Jesus was speaking of the rock of Peter's confession, the truth that Jesus is the Christ. But this is not the same Greek word that Peter chose to use in 2:4–12. Instead, Peter chose the word *stone* (*lithos*) five times (note that the word is not used in the Greek in the first part of verse 7) and the word *rock* (*petra*) only once (2:8). Although the Greek word may be different, the purpose of the word is the same: to show that Jesus Christ is the rock-solid foundation of the Christian church. Peter used the word from his Scriptures (*lithos*) in verses 4 and 5 as he set the stage to reveal to us the nature of the church that is built on Christ. There can be little doubt that Matthew 16 was on his mind as he wrote. Christ certainly will build His church and the gates of hell will not prevail against it.

The Character of the Church (1 Pet. 2:4–5)

There is no single metaphor that adequately describes the character of Christ. He is described as living water (John 4:10–14; 7:38), living bread (John 6:51), a living way (John 5:26), and here in 1 Peter 2:4 as a **living Stone**. He is **living** not just because He has risen from the dead to die no more, but because He is life itself (John 1:4) and the source of life for all who would come to Him. Although He was **rejected by men**, He was **chosen by**

God and precious to him (1 Pet. 2:4). The word translated **precious** (also used in v. 6) literally means "honored, prized, or highly esteemed." Here we see the reversal of values: What is highly honored and esteemed by God is often rejected and hated by people. Thus, we can never use the world's standard as a measure of our success or acceptance by God.

The description of Jesus is given as a means of comparison. Peter said that his readers were **like living stones** (v. 5), because they derived their life from Christ. They belong to Him and reflect His character as they hold out life to a lost world. And like Christ, they will be rejected by people. At this time in history, persecution under Nero was increasing among Christians. A sub-theme of 1 Peter is suffering, and it is obvious that Peter's readers were undergoing great trials because of their faith in Christ. (See 2:12; 3:14–17; 4:4, 12–19.) They were no different from their Master; though they were rejected by people, they were esteemed and honored by God.

As **living stones**, though, they were **being built into a spiritual house** (2:5). Notice that they are not the ones doing the building. They **are being built**. This is a picture of a process initiated and implemented by God. As people come to Christ, they become part of His church, stones carefully hewn by the Architect and wisely interconnected to build a house. But not just any house. They become a **spiritual house**. The reference is obviously to the temple, which was still standing at the time Peter wrote this letter in the early A.D. 60s and which was but a foreshadow of the coming church. The temple was the place where God's presence dwelt, the place where people came to worship, the place that was holy, set apart for God. The church becomes the dwelling place of God. Together we become His temple. (See 1 Cor. 3:16.)

Thoughts of the temple naturally give rise to the worship that was offered there, prompting Peter's description of the church as **a holy priesthood, offering spiritual sacrifices** (1 Pet. 2:5). Just as the Old Testament priests were wholly dedicated to the service of the Lord and set apart for His service, so it should be with the church. In Old Testament times, the average person was unable to enter into the presence of the Lord in the Most Holy Place, a privilege reserved for only the high priest once a year. But now, as **a holy priesthood**, every single believer has access to the throne of God in prayer through the blood of Christ. (See Heb. 10:19.)

Unlike the Old Testament priests who offered animal sacrifices to atone for sin and to express their dedication to God, the sacrifices the Christian church is to offer are spiritual in nature. We are to offer our bodies (Rom. 12:1) and our sincere praises and good deeds (Heb. 13:15–16). Such sacrifices are **acceptable to God through Jesus Christ** (1 Pet. 2:5). It is only because of His perfect and final sacrifice through His death on the cross, which put an end forever to the necessity of the Old Testament sacrificial system, that our offerings are acceptable to God.

WORDS FROM WESLEY

1 Peter 2:5

To the same effect St. Peter says, "Ye are a holy priesthood, to offer up spiritual sacrifices, acceptable to God through Jesus Christ." But what sacrifices shall we offer now, seeing the Jewish dispensation is at an end? If you have truly presented yourselves to God, you offer up to Him continually all your thoughts, and words, and actions, through the Son of His love, as a sacrifice of praise and thanksgiving. (WJW, vol. 6, 414)

The church becomes a reflection of Christ, as living stones, and becomes a temple where His presence dwells. But this happens only **as you come to him** (v. 4). The participle used here is plural, indicating that this is only possible as we come to Christ together, united. The verb is also in the present tense, which means it is a habitual, continual drawing near to God. Both personally and corporately we are to enjoy close fellowship and communion with Christ, a relationship that must be nurtured continually, habitually, and intentionally. Only then can we truly be the church.

The Foundation of the Church (1 Pet. 2:6–8)

In these next verses, Peter quoted three passages from the Septuagint: Isaiah 28:16; Psalm 118:22; and Isaiah 8:14. These verses reveal the foundation of the church: belief in Jesus Christ. Jesus is described in Isaiah 28:16 as a **cornerstone** (1 Pet. 2:6), the huge stone that anchored the building and determined its design and orientation. It is an apt description of Jesus Christ, who is the anchor for our faith and the foundation of everything we believe. The cornerstone was always **chosen and precious** (v. 6), carefully selected at great cost. Jesus, too, was chosen and infinitely precious. The church is built on the foundation of Christ and comprises those who believe in Him.

There are only two responses to Christ: trust or rejection. **The one who trusts in him will never be put to shame** (v. 6). Those who *believe* (the actual Greek word used here) in Christ will not be disgraced or dishonored (most likely speaking of their position before God, not before people). In the NIV, verse 7 is translated, **Now to you who believe, this stone is precious**, although the word **stone** is not in the Greek text. The word translated **precious** is not the same word that is used in verses 4 and 6. Instead, this word means "honor." The sentence is difficult to translate, but it may mean something closer to "Unto you who believe is the honor," which would fit perfectly with the preceding verse. We receive honor from God for putting our trust in Christ.

But to those who do not believe (v. 7) the position is quite the opposite. The stone they rejected has become the **capstone** (literally "the head of the corner" or cornerstone), just as we saw in verse 4. That **stone . . . causes men to stumble** (v. 8) and will result in ultimate judgment, bringing their downfall. Those who disobey are **destined for** judgment (v. 8); it is the predetermined result of their choice to reject Christ.

The Practice of the Church (1 Pet. 2:9–10)

Peter's audience was "God's elect" (1:1), and he was confident that they were among those who placed their trust in Christ. They **are a chosen people** (2:9), just as the nation of Israel had been chosen to be His representatives on earth and to be the recipients of His blessings. But not all who were born into Israel were truly Israel (see Rom. 9:6–8)—only those who lived in obedience to God. In the same way, only those who have a saving relationship with Christ are part of the true church. Peter deliberately used Old Testament terminology that referred to Israel to now designate the position of the church. It may be merely as an example, or it may be an indication that Peter saw the church as the fulfillment of Israel. Indeed, Paul said in Ephesians 3:6 that Gentiles and Israel are heirs together and members of one body (not that there are two ways to heaven, but both come to Christ and together they become God's chosen people), and in Galatians 3:28, "There is neither Jew nor Greek, slave nor free, male nor female, for you are all one in Christ Jesus."

Peter also identified the church as **a royal priesthood, a holy nation, a people belonging to God** (1 Pet. 2:9), designations commonly used in the Old Testament to refer to Israel. We are **royal** in that we have become the dwelling place of the King of Kings and somehow share in His kingship. We are **holy** and owned by God. (See 1 Pet. 1:15; 1 Cor. 6:20.)

Notice that there is a purpose for the church. Who they are (and whose they are) influences what they do: **that you may declare the praises of him who called you out of darkness into his wonderful light** (1 Pet. 2:9). The church is to declare His **praises**, a word that means a "virtues" or "excellencies." As the church, our practice should be an advertisement of God's virtue. Our conduct should sing His praises.

WORDS FROM WESLEY

1 Peter 2:9

But ye—Who believe in Christ, *are*—In a higher sense than ever the Jews were, *a chosen* or elect *race, a royal priesthood*—Kings and priests unto God (Rev. 1:6). As princes, ye have power with God, and victory over sin, the world, and the devil: as priests, ye are consecrated to God, for offering spiritual sacrifices. Ye Christians are as one *holy nation*—Under Christ your King, *a purchased people*—Who are His peculiar property; *that ye may show forth*—By your whole behaviour to all mankind; *the virtues*—The excellent glory, the mercy, wisdom, and power *of him*—Christ, *who hath called you out of the darkness*—Of ignorance, error, sin, and misery. (ENNT)

Our desire and obligation to live such a life (both individually and corporately) stems from our gratitude for what He has done for us. He has **called you out of darkness into his wonderful light** (v. 9), and **once you were not a people, but now you are the people of God; once you had not received mercy, but now you have received mercy** (v. 10). We were recipients of God's mercy when we gave our lives to Him and He saved us from our sins. God took us out of darkness and into the light of Christ at that very moment (Eph. 5:8) and adopted us into His family (John 1:12). In view of such mercy, the only appropriate response is a life of holiness.

WORDS FROM WESLEY

1 Peter 2:11

Sojourners, pilgrims—The first word properly means, those who are in a strange house: the second, those who are in a strange country. You sojourn in the body: you are pilgrims in this world: abstain from desires of any thing in this house, or in this country. (ENNT)

The Witness of the Church (1 Pet. 2:11–12)

Peter urged his readers to live **as aliens and strangers in the world** (v. 11). **Aliens** had no rights or legal status; **strangers** were only temporary residents. Christians are to be in the world but not of the world. (See John 17:14–16.) They should see heaven as their home and their goal. By doing so, Christians become a witness in the world. They will **abstain from sinful desires** and **live . . . good lives among the pagans** (vv. 11–12) (the word translated **good** literally means "honest"). In their private lives they will abstain from doing what's wrong, and in their public lives they will determine to do what is good, upright, and honest, with the end result that **they may see your good deeds and glorify God on the day he visits us** (v. 12).

WORDS FROM WESLEY
1 Peter 2:12

Honest—Not barely unblameable, but virtuous in every respect. But our language sinks under the force, beauty, and copiousness of the original expressions: *that they by your good works which they shall behold*—See with their own eyes, *may glorify God*—By owning His grace in you, and following your example: *in the day of visitation*—The time when He shall give them fresh offers of His mercy. (ENNT)

The rest of 1 Peter expands on these last two verses, sharing practical ways of being a light to a darkened world. This is what it means to be living stones: sharing the life of Christ with a world that needs the true living Stone. When we follow the principles found in 1 Peter 2:4–12, we become a church that is empowered by God, a church that will prevail over the gates of hell because Jesus Christ is our rock and all that we do flows from our relationship with Him.

DISCUSSION

Peter offered a thought-provoking image of the community of faith as a collection of living stones being built into a house on the foundation of the Lord Jesus Christ.

1. Peter described members of the church as precious stones. What parallels do you see between precious stones and the church?

2. Old Testament priests represented God to the people and people to God. How is it possible that all believers are now priests? What implications does this hold for your personal spiritual life?

3. What do you think spiritual sacrifices are? What would make such sacrifices "acceptable"?

4. A capstone holds the two opposing sides of an arch together. If Jesus is our capstone, list some ways that He brings unity to the church—your local congregation, your larger denominational fellowship, and the church around the world.

5. What would cause some people to see Jesus as a capstone and others to view Him as a stumbling block? Which view do you think is most prevalent in your community? How do you see that evidenced?

6. Christians are described as aliens or foreigners in the world. If we were to adopt that attitude about ourselves, what changes might we make in our lifestyle or attitudes?

7. What does it mean to live in darkness? How can we lead those in darkness into the light?

PRAYER

Most merciful God, please help us understand the depth of Your mercy toward us. Open our eyes to the magnitude of Your grace and the glorious life we have in You. May we immediately flee from anything that might make war against our souls, the very souls for which You sacrificed Your Son to save.

4

POWER IN SUBMISSION

1 Peter 2:13—3:7

When we show respect for authority, we follow the example of Christ.

It may seem contradictory to speak the words *power* and *submission* in the same phrase. They seem to be opposites or at least unrelated; but in the Christian sense, they are two sides of the same coin. Peter saw submission as a great source of power in the relationships of the believer. He gave us insight into three aspects of life as he opened up this wonderful concept. Christian citizens, Christian slaves (employees), and Christian spouses are all challenged by the apostle to live lives of submission and thus follow the example of Christ himself.

When worldly people dream and seek power, they establish tyranny, build empires, and grab at authority. When Christians think of power, they seek to gain positive influence, engender respect, and strengthen bonds of love. The indwelling Holy Spirit teaches us and grows within us a proper understanding of what power is all about—enabling others to be and become all that God can make them to be. That is the essence of power in the Christian life, and in this study, the Holy Spirit, through the apostle Peter, gives us great insight into developing this type of power.

COMMENTARY

Already in the first century, Christians were beginning to be noticed because they did not offer sacrifices to the pagan gods of the cities they lived in. Of special concern to Roman officials was the Christians' refusal to offer annual sacrifices in the emperor's honor, praying for his health and well-being. In the eyes of Rome, this was treason. Persecution of Christians was neither systematic nor widespread, but for this and other reasons, Christians had cause to be watchful.

"The power of submission" is a good focus for this passage, for Peter and the vast majority of Christians saw their calling in Christ to be peacemakers. They had no intention of plotting or initiating treason against their Roman masters, even though most Christians were not Roman citizens. This is a good word for our culture, too, as it understands almost nothing of submission, except by force—which is useless for growth in maturity. Not even our Christian culture today understands the tremendous power of submission—whether individually or as the whole body of Christ—to effect change within and without the body, in persons and in institutions.

Submission to Public Authority (1 Pet. 2:13–17)

Submit yourselves (v. 13) is the operative command for Christians here. It does *not* say, "See that someone else submits to you." The command is incumbent upon each of us to submit to others, *reciprocally*, for reasons Peter made clear as he advanced his argument and instruction throughout the passage.

What we are to submit ourselves to should be rendered (with NASB) "to every human institution," *not* **authority** (v. 13). Greek *ktisis* is, in every other New Testament occurrence, rendered "creation," "created being/order," and so forth. God intended righteous institutions, justly administered, as good gifts for the beneficial ordering of culture and the protection of people—individuals and groups—from the unrighteous exercise of power. That God-created mandate and responsibility, *not* **authority**, is Peter's focus here.

The rest of the passage consists in examples of Christian submission **for the Lord's sake** (v. 13), beginning with **the king, as the supreme authority**, and **governors, who are sent by** the king (vv. 13–14). Of course, we must understand this for the political system of Peter's day, and then consider how we should conduct ourselves within the framework of the radically different political systems of our own day. *Because* the Christian faith tends toward human freedom, *because* the West was Christian for more than fifteen hundred years, and *because* the world has made democracy the political touchstone over the last century, the supreme political authority no longer rests with kings, but with the people. Does that change Peter's instructions here?

In at least one respect, no. Democracies are not anarchies. We elect persons to represent us, enact laws, and set policies; others are appointed or hired to help in the process. Christians should respect and heed all these people, so long as the laws and policies do not violate God's higher law. In that sense, Peter's instruction still applies.

But Christians belong to the body politic in representative democracies. We have a duty to be informed citizens and to be vigilant in the defense of our freedom, which is both God's gift and the natural result of the spread of our Judeo-Christian heritage across our world today. It is even more important to be involved citizens as we see Western culture increasingly turn away from the God in whom our freedom is found.

God's will is **by doing good** to **silence the ignorant talk of foolish men**, or unthinking persons (v. 15). In Peter's day, unthinking persons naturally followed their civilized pagan culture in believing that pagan sacrifices were the way to demonstrate loyalty to Caesar. Christians could silence unthinking criticism of their loyalty to God who forbids sacrifices to other gods, by being law-abiding, model subjects widely known for doing right and good.

Verse 16 is a continuation of the previous sentence; it builds to a startling climax by the use of a radical paradox. Christians are to **live as free** persons and also **as servants of God**. As a social, political reality, most Christians were not free persons in Peter's day. Yet, in Christ, they were free, and Peter exhorted them to live that way. At the same time, being free in Christ, they were **servants of God**, and should live as such. That paradox enabled the early Christians to exercise their freedom for a set of goods (allegiances, values, lifestyles, and outcomes), rather than **as a cover-up for evil**, which is not liberty, but license (v. 16).

WORDS FROM WESLEY

1 Peter 2:17

Be double honour paid,
To man beloved of God,
Man in his Maker's image made,
And purchased by His blood:
Mark'd with Thy character,
Lord, every soul is Thine,
And I in all mankind revere
Their Ransomer Divine. (PW, vol. 13, 180)

Peter summed up this general responsibility of the Christian in a series of four commands. **Show proper respect to everyone** is in the future tense, implying this is a permanent duty and privilege of the Christian. **Love the brotherhood of believers** and **fear** (revere) **God** (v. 17). One might expect believers to do this as a matter of course, though we all know these are sometimes easier or harder to do.

The final command, **honor the king** (v. 17), is the same verb as the first one, but here it is in the present tense. Peter must have intended the change of tense, and the resulting contrast. All humans are to be honored, all the time and everywhere, because all reflect the image of the God who created them. But a king's rule is only temporary. Christians, together with all loyal subjects, owe the king this honor, but it is last on the list, and of the four commands, is the only one to be temporally framed.

WORDS FROM WESLEY

1 Peter 2:17

My heart is harden'd from Thy fear,
Till Thou the stone remove,
Till love constrain me to revere
The God of pardoning love:
Father, declare Thyself to me
Through Jesus reconciled,
Then shall I always render Thee
The reverence of a child. (PW, vol. 13, 180)

Submission Inspired By Jesus' Example (1 Pet. 2:18–25)

A despicable institution of Peter's day was human slavery. But slave revolts were neither effective, nor were they God's way of changing the system to eliminate this evil institution. For Peter's day, God's instruction was, **Slaves, submit yourselves to your masters** (v. 18).

Submission was at least tolerable under a master who was **good and considerate.** But what about those who were **harsh** (v. 18; literally, "crooked" or "unjust")? Would not a slave be justified in slacking, and in sneaky sabotage of such a master's interests?

Peter argued that, however justified it might seem (or even be), a tit-for-tat response to a master's unjust cruelty would play into the master's hands (v. 20). It would justify the master's injustice, even though after the fact.

But suffering injustice because one is **conscious of God** is **commendable before God** (vv. 19–20). Peter stated this principle strongly, essentially saying, "This is grace." How good to do something that is "grace, in God's judgment"! This is true because in suffering injustice without retaliation we follow the example of Christ himself. **Example** (v. 21) is literally "pattern" or "model."

Verse 22 is a quotation of Isaiah 53:9. Peter's use of **sin** for the original usually rendered "violence" is appropriate for the context of his argument here.

The rest of this paragraph (vv. 23–25) also has its source in Isaiah 53, though it is not all verbatim. Peter's first point was to emphasize that Jesus in no way retaliated for the many injustices done to Him in the course of His arrest, trial, and crucifixion. For that reason, and that alone, we should endure our own suffering without retaliation or revenge.

WORDS FROM WESLEY

1 Peter 2:24

Who himself bore our sins—That is, the punishment due to them, in His afflicted, torn, dying *body on the tree*—The cross, whereon chiefly slaves or servants were wont to suffer; *that we being dead to sin*—Wholly delivered both from the guilt and power of it: (indeed without an atonement first made for the guilt, we could never have been delivered from the power) *might live to righteousness*—Which is one only. The sins we had committed, and He bore, were manifold. (ENNT)

But Peter's second point gives an even greater meaning to such suffering of injustice; in God's paradoxical eternal economy, unjust suffering willingly endured pays enormous dividends. Here Peter emphasized—by placing them at the end, the climax, of his paragraph—three great benefits Christ's suffering gained for those who place their faith in Him. We **die to sins and live for righteousness** (v. 24). **By his wounds** we **have been healed** (v. 24). No more **like sheep going astray . . . now** we **have returned to the Shepherd and Overseer of** our **souls** (v. 25).

It is amazing that Christ's suffering of injustice should have gained so much good for those who trust in Him. It also is amazing to think that our own suffering of injustice may work for good and for grace to others, as well as ourselves. But such is Peter's claim, and such is the witness of Christians' faithful living and dying across the centuries.

Submission to One's Spouse (1 Pet. 3:1–7)

In the same way (v. 1) is the key phrase to notice in this paragraph if Christian husbands wish to avoid becoming like the unjust masters Peter just spoke of. Autocracy, slavery, and patriarchy were facts of life in Peter's Greco-Roman world. That does not make any of these institutions God-ordained or right. Peter's counsel here concerns how Christians are to live as a godly minority in an ungodly world, trammeled by ungodly institutions.

In the same way (v. 1) wives were to offer willing submission to their husbands within the framework of their patriarchal society. The result (not inevitable, but not uncommon either) would be that husbands who **do not believe the Word . . . may be won over without words**. This is not a command to husbands to lord over their wives. It is an exhortation to wives to win unbelieving husbands by the same means that slaves might win over unjust masters—by submitting to intrinsically unjust institutions and patterns of behavior for the greater goal, the possible salvation of their masters or husbands.

This spirit of submission for the greater good exhibits itself in a **beauty** that is not merely **outward adornment** (v. 3). This verse is not a prohibition of **braided hair and the wearing of gold jewelry and fine clothes**, as has often been taught. It is a warning to women, and men as well, not to become so shallow that we think our good looks come from such adornment. Real loveliness is **the unfading beauty of a gentle and quiet spirit** (v. 4). If we understand and practice that, we will not go wrong in the wearing of outward apparel and adornment.

WORDS FROM WESLEY

1 Peter 3:3

The wearing gay or costly apparel naturally tends to breed and to increase vanity. By vanity I here mean, the love and desire of being admired and praised. Every one of you that is fond of dress has a witness of this in your own bosom. Whether you will confess it before man or no, you are convinced of this before God. You know in your hearts, it is with a view to be admired that you thus adorn yourselves; and that you would not be at the pains were none to see you but God and His holy angels. Now, the more you indulge this foolish desire, the more it grows upon you. You have vanity enough by nature; but by thus indulging it, you increase it a hundred-fold. O stop! Aim at pleasing God alone, and all these ornaments will drop off. (WJW, vol. 7, 18–19)

Should wives submit to their husbands? Of course they should. And **in the same way** (v. 7) husbands should submit to their wives. In Peter's day, a husband's submission to his wife lay in the fact that he was to treat her "according to knowledge," the knowledge revealed in Christ's redemptive work for us that all humans are created in God's image. That meant that the Christian husband was to live counterculturally with his wife in the deeply patriarchal systems of the day.

In ancient Asia Minor, as in our own cultural patterns, to live biblically very often means to live clearly and conspicuously across the grain of the culture's sin-subverted and merely temporal values. The only way we can do that consistently is to heed Peter's counsel and follow in the steps of Jesus Christ himself.

DISCUSSION

While the world is engaged in a never-ending power grab, Jesus called His disciples to follow Him in serving rather than being served. So Peter taught his readers the surprising power in submission.

1. What are Peter's instructions to various groups concerning submission to authority? What parts did you find surprising?

2. According to Peter, what is the value of government? Is that value still present when the state is guilty of wrongdoing?

3. What would it mean to live as free people when the people were under the domination of a foreign power?

4. What would it mean to show proper respect and honor for the king when living under a corrupt political system? What ways of showing respect would be acceptable for Christians?

5. Is willingly accepting punishment for disobeying an unjust law an act of insubordination to the government? Is that showing respect or not?

6. Which issues facing your society cause you to be angry or feel helpless? In what ways have you considered responding to those issues?

7. Based on these verses, what advice would you give to a person who believed his or her country was involved in an unjust war? What advice would you give to a person who believed his or her government was being oppressed by a foreign power?

PRAYER

Most merciful Savior, please teach us to be humble servants, that we might have the strength of submission we need to bring glory to You and Your kingdom from this day forward and forevermore.

5

EXPERIENCING RESURRECTION POWER

1 Peter 3:8–22

The resurrection of Jesus Christ empowers Christians today.

Jesus Christ had been crucified. His dead body had been removed from the cross and placed in the burial tomb belonging to Joseph of Arimathea. The large stone, which was rolled in front of the entrance, was an indication of the finality of the event. The soldiers who were present at the crucifixion as well as Jesus' followers could testify that Jesus Christ was dead.

On the first day of the week, while darkness still blanketed the hills, Mary Magdalene went to look at the tomb where Jesus' body had been placed. What she saw caused her to panic. The large entrance stone had been rolled away. Her first thought was that someone had come and had stolen the body (John 20:2). When Peter heard Mary's report, he ran to the tomb to verify for himself what she had said. Only days later did Peter understand that though Jesus had been crucified, He was alive!

Now Peter wrote to communicate the power of this incredible truth to Christians who have not had the privilege of seeing the resurrected Lord. This study makes the good news come alive for any who have not heard it or who have lost the excitement and wonder of this cornerstone event in the Christian story.

COMMENTARY

This study builds on the passage of the previous concerning appropriate submission for the greater good. The emphasis in this latter part of chapter 3 is not on submission, per se, but on the broader issue of what makes godly character. If suffering follows from being righteous, so be it. In this, as in all things, we have Christ as our example. But more, we have Christ as our champion, as Peter went on to discuss briefly at the end of the chapter.

A Profile of the Godly Person (1 Pet. 3:8–12)

Finally (v. 8) refers to the connection of this section with the previous section on mutual or reciprocal submission. What does submission, looking out for the best interests of others, look like? Peter had discussed it briefly, with respect to rulers, masters, and spouses. Now he summed it up by listing six virtues.

These six virtues are not just actions to perform or even attitudes to assume. They are characteristics by which a person can and should come to be defined and recognized. Grammatically, these six words actually are participles, a form that stresses their "beingness," their integrity to the character and demeanor, of the person exhibiting them: Be harmonious, **be sympathetic**, be lovers of the brother/sisterhood, **be compassionate**, be **humble** (v. 8); after another participle with a negative (**do not repay**), be a blessing (v. 9).

WORDS FROM WESLEY

1 Peter 3:8

Sympathizing—Rejoicing and sorrowing together: *love*—All believers *as brethren, be pitiful*—Towards the afflicted; *be courteous*—To all men. Courtesy is, such a behaviour towards equals and inferiors, as shows respect mixed with love. (ENNT)

Further, all six are relational virtues. They are exhibited only in the company, and in appropriate deference and ministry to the legitimate needs, of other persons.

The participle with a negative, **Do not repay** (v. 9), interrupts the chain just before its climax. This serves two purposes (at least). By interrupting a chain of positives, the destructiveness of the negatives is thrown into sharper relief. It simply does not become the follower of Christ, characterized by these six radiant virtues, to **repay evil with evil** (v. 9). Conversely, when the sixth virtue is commanded, **but with blessing**, its goodness contrasts with great impact the pettiness and destructiveness of the course Peter just had urged his readers and hearers to renounce.

Second, the interruption heightens anticipation of the sixth virtue by delaying its disclosure momentarily. In this way, "be a blessing" (see v. 9) is revealed as the climactic positive good of the six virtues Peter urged. In the context of the immediately preceding negative, we should understand "be a blessing" here as "be doing a good turn for, or speaking a blessing upon rather than taking revenge in action or in speech."

Peter's final statement here is really quite astonishing. We are to bless, even in the face of insult, **because to this you were called so that you may inherit a blessing** (v. 9). The believer's destiny is to receive blessing unimaginable this side of eternity. The best preparation for that is to practice blessing, even including those who do not bless us.

Peter reinforced his point by a long quotation, Psalm 34:12–16. In this case of a Psalm quoted for the benefit of readers and hearers who included many Jewish persons, it probably was not necessary to cite the passage; many of them would have known from where Peter was quoting.

Life and **good days** (1 Pet. 3:10) we may think of as a kind of Old Testament shorthand for the blessing of which Peter just had spoken in verse 9. The character and demeanor necessary to enjoy these (that is, to enjoy the blessing) are reflected in the avoidance of evil and the pursuit of good and peace that are the subject of the remainder of verses 10 and 11. This is the same character Peter was describing and urging with his list of the six virtues; the quotation is his scriptural warrant for urging believers to attain to them.

The eyes of the Lord are on the righteous (v. 12) means God watches over the righteous for their protection and good. Together with God's hearing **their prayer**, God's watchfulness means the righteous will enjoy the **life** and **good days** they desire (v. 10). This may not always be true in a material sense, but it always is true in the best, and certainly in an eternal, sense.

Suffering for the Right (1 Pet. 3:13–17)

The question, **Who is going to harm you if you are eager to do good?** (v. 13), is rhetorical. **Eager** translates the Greek word from which we get our English *zealous* (as NASB renders it). The expected answer to this rhetorical question is "No one!" In the vast majority of cases, it also is the correct answer. Pressure to conform, as exerted by society at large, usually supports the kind of behavior Peter urged upon his readers here.

But Peter understood that, in fact, the righteous sometimes do suffer injustice at the hands of the wicked. What then? **You are blessed** (v. 14). Peter already had said in 2:20 that for one suffering unjustly, "this is commendable before God." It is no small thing to enjoy favor with God!

In your hearts set apart Christ as Lord (3:15) is the positive action that makes it possible to face down fear and dread. Those who cause believers to suffer unjustly cannot take away from them their dedication to God, which consecrates the suffering as an offering that God accepts as of great value. In that way, the suffering the wicked intended for evil works rather to the eternal good of the righteous.

If the righteous suffer in this manner, inevitably some will wonder how they can do it, and why they would. **To give an answer** (v. 15) renders the Greek word from which we get English *apologetics*, the area of biblical and theological knowledge and doctrine concerned with explaining the Christian faith to nonbelievers. Peter declared that even those suffering persecution for the name of Christ should be ready to explain their faith to their tormenters or any others who may ask.

Gentleness and respect, keeping a clear conscience (vv. 15–16) are important even when experiencing the trauma of unjust suffering. They are important to one's own well-being, but that is not Peter's focus. Even here, the Christian should submit to others—in this situation, to wicked others—in order that one's revilers **may be ashamed of their slander** (v. 16). Peter did not say it here, but one implication is that perhaps they may be convicted and even converted through this blameless witness.

We should understand **if it is God's will** (v. 17) as referring to God's permissive will, God's usual stance of allowing humans to choose and follow their own course, even when we choose evil. (God does woo us toward himself and toward good, but He usually does not directly restrain humans from doing evil.) If, then, evil persons are going to inflict suffering upon us, and God does not intervene to spare us, it is better to suffer because we are good than because we ourselves are evil. Then, too, in a just society, evildoers suffer consequences for their evildoing. It is better, if suffering is to be our lot, to suffer at the hands of evil persons because of our good character, than to suffer at the hands of righteous persons, charged with safeguarding society, for the evil that we do. In all circumstances and for all reasons, Peter urged the believer to choose the good, regardless of whether suffering follows.

Christ Our Example and Champion (1 Pet. 3:18–22)

Peter then took his discourse in a startling new direction, comparing what we may potentially suffer with what Christ already has suffered. Peter was not saying that our suffering will have the same effect as Christ's suffering. But if we should suffer, it is to be in the spirit of Christ who suffered, **the righteous for the unrighteous** (v. 18). If Christ was willing to suffer that way, should not His followers also be willing?

Christ died for sins once for all (v. 18). This statement refers to the New Testament conviction and teaching that Jesus was God's perfect sacrifice for sin. The Levitical system of animal and grain sacrifices was a temporary measure, and a teaching exercise, to help God's people learn that sin and its alienation carry a huge price tag, one that ultimately only Jesus could pay. But when He did pay that price, by being **put to death in the body** (v. 18), other sacrifices no longer were necessary or useful. Because this was a central teaching of the early church, here Peter had only to make reference to it in the phrase **once for all** (v. 18), and his readers and hearers knew what he meant.

WORDS FROM WESLEY

1 Peter 3:18

For—This is undoubtedly best, whereby we are most conformed to Christ. *Now Christ suffered once*—To suffer no more, *for sins*—Not His own, but ours; *the just for the unjust*—The word signifies, not only them who have wronged their neighbours, but those who have transgressed any of the commands of God: as the preceding word *just* denotes a person who has fulfilled, not barely social duties, but all kinds of righteousness: *that he might bring us to God*—Now to His gracious favour, hereafter to His blissful presence, by the same steps, of suffering and of glory: *being put to death in the flesh*—As man, *but raised to life by the Spirit*—Both by His own divine power, and by the power of the Holy Ghost. (ENNT)

Peter then took a little detour praise, as it were, mentioning some lesser-known features of Jesus' sacrificial death and its meaning. Having been **made alive by the Spirit** (v. 18), He **went and preached to the spirits in prison** (v. 19). Who were these spirits? Peter's answer is the only biblical reference to a possible alternative fate of those who ignored or rejected God's Word: **Noah while the ark was being built** (v. 20).

Peter's reference to **prison** (v. 19) has long fascinated Bible readers. He probably had in mind *Sheol*, the most common Hebrew term for the place of the dead. Until late in the Old Testament period, at least, there does not seem to have been a developed theology of the final destination of the righteous dead as a place distinct from that of the wicked dead.

WORDS FROM WESLEY

1 Peter 3:19

By which Spirit he preached—Through the ministry of Noah, *to the spirits in prison*—The unholy men before the flood; who were then reserved by the justice of God as in a prison, till He executed the sentence upon them all: and are now also reserved to the judgment of the great day. (ENNT)

Does Jesus' preaching to these people from the ancient world imply their salvation at this time? Possibly. Does it guarantee their salvation? No more than all those who heard Jesus preach during the years of His earthly ministry.

Peter's real point in this short digression also leads in the opposite direction. He mentioned those who perished, to bring into his discussion the **eight** persons **saved through water** (v. 20). Their salvation in water is the type, of which our own baptism is the fulfillment. We are not baptized for **the removal of dirt from the body but** for **a good conscience toward God** (v. 21).

Peter then reached the climax of his "praise detour." He affirmed in jubilant tones **the resurrection of Jesus Christ** (v. 21), and Jesus' subsequent exaltation in heaven, **at God's right hand** (v. 22). Not as though anything were needed beyond that to complete Jesus' triumph, but as a further consequence of His total victory over the forces of evil, **angels, authorities and powers** are **in submission to him** (v. 22). These three groups are not the focus here but, rather, the completeness of Jesus' triumph. It is His triumph that the church celebrates ever since in the weekly Lord's Day worship and more especially in the annual jubilation of Easter Sunday, when we affirm with utmost joy, "Christ is risen! He is risen, indeed!"

WORDS FROM WESLEY
1 Peter 3:21

Through the water of baptism we are saved from the sin which overwhelms the world as a flood; not indeed the bare outward sign, but the inward grace; a divine consciousness, that both our persons and our actions are accepted, through Him who died and rose again for us. (ENNT)

And with this, Peter now had come full circle in the development of his teaching on the subject of submission, which he had begun in 2:13. Jesus triumphed through learning submission by way of the cross, and now all are subject to Him. Peter urged Jesus' followers to learn submission in a variety of circumstances for a variety of good ends, not the least of which is that we, too, may have a share in Jesus' triumph when He says in the end, "Well done, good and faithful servant! . . . Come and share your master's happiness!" (Matt. 25:21).

DISCUSSION

The crucifixion and resurrection of Jesus are the heart of the gospel—the good news that Jesus is Lord. The resurrection assures the believer that God's new creation is already in progress.

1. Some Christians teach that believers who have enough faith are rewarded by God with lives of ease and comfort. Do you believe that is true? What evidence supports your view?

2. Describe Christ's attitude toward suffering?

3. List the benefits of suffering that you see described in 1 Peter 3:8–22. What else comes to mind based on other Scriptures?

4. What role can suffering play in the development of holiness?

5. Why would nonbelievers "heap abuse" on Christians? Describe instances of this, either from history or from your own experience.

6. How does suffering make it difficult to remain clear minded and self-controlled (see vv. 15–16)?

7. Based on these verses, what advice would you give to someone who is suffering?

8. Describe the role of the church in coping with suffering? What examples have you seen of how the fellowship of Christians relieves suffering?

9. What does it mean to faithfully administer God's grace in its various forms to those who are suffering? In what was does your church or small group do this? In what ways are you involved?

10. What could your church or small group do to relieve the suffering of those within your church? In your community? In other countries?

PRAYER

Most powerful God, please engrain in us the indelible power of the resurrection, that we may never return evil with evil but always be willing to suffer for doing what is right.

6

EVIDENCE OF A CHANGED LIFE

1 Peter 4:1–11

Salvation produces life transformation.

Jesus Christ intended the church to be light and salt in the world. Therefore, Christians stand in stark contrast to the darkness and corruption of the world system in which they are placed. The world order has tried to squeeze Christians into its mold. Our challenge is to keep the contrast sharp by maintaining our distinctive inner life and outer character.

The display on a church bulletin board read, "If you were accused of being a Christian, would there be enough evidence to convict you?" Too often, the answer would be no. It is all too easy for peer pressures, career stresses, family problems, or just plain selfishness to weigh against our claim that we are Christians.

In this study, however, Peter told us how to win that conviction by giving evidence of our faith through a changed life. He issued a clear challenge to steadfastly resist the power of darkness that seeks to erase the line of demarcation between the church and the world.

COMMENTARY

Peter's purpose in writing his letter was to challenge his readers to apply God's grace to their perilous situation and to encourage and comfort them with the living hope that comes with true commitment to Christ. Likewise, his words encourage us as we live in a contemporary society where standing for Christ causes us to be misunderstood, belittled, ostracized, and hurt.

Arm Yourself with an Attitude (1 Pet. 4:1–2)

Christ is our example of suffering. As we look at Christ's life and death, we find that He suffered in every aspect as we do and even to a greater degree. Yet despite all, Christ never sinned. He completely yielded himself to the Father's will (Matt. 26:39; Phil. 2:5–8). Peter was encouraging believers to look at Jesus and adopt a similar attitude. **Arm yourselves also with the same attitude** (1 Pet. 4:1), for the battles of life are won or lost because of our attitudes. Behavior is dictated by how we think. It is not the crisis we face that is important but our attitude in that situation.

WORDS FROM WESLEY

1 Peter 4:2

Namely, all real Christians, or believers in Christ, are made free from outward sin. And the same freedom, which St. Paul here expresses in such variety of phrases, St. Peter expresses in that one (1 Pet. 4:1–2): "He that hath suffered in the flesh, hath ceased from sin—that he no longer should live to the desires of men, but to the will of God." For this *ceasing from sin*, if it be interpreted in the lowest sense, as regarding only the outward behaviour, must denote the ceasing from the outward act, from any outward transgression of the law. (WJW, vol. 6, 7)

Dare to Be Different (1 Pet. 4:3–6)

For you have spent enough time in the past doing what pagans choose to do (v. 3). No matter how young or how old we are when we come to Christ, we feel that our pre-Christ days were wasted. Yes, how many blessings from God have we sacrificed on the altars of our pagan lifestyles?

Peter outlined the pagan lifestyle with a list of behaviors including **debauchery, lust, drunkenness, orgies, carousing and . . . idolatry** (v. 3). A more contemporary list may include illicit sex, violence, drugs, and alcohol. Although many people may not have been deeply involved in these kinds of behaviors, nevertheless we all can identify with being selfish, self-indulgent, self-centered, self-driven, self-sufficient, and so on. Whenever we are living for self, we are actually living a pagan lifestyle.

Is it any wonder that when we begin to live unselfishly by putting Christ and others first, those who are entrenched in worldly behaviors do not understand us? They feel threatened when we have no desire for their self-indulgent pleasures.

So what gives us the courage to withstand their ridicule and abuse? **But they will have to give account to him who is ready to judge the living and the dead** (v. 5). The truth is that everyone must give an account of his or her life before the One who is the final Judge. Knowing there is a day of accountability will keep us striving to live for Jesus. If we are to follow Christ's example, we must dare to be different.

WORDS FROM WESLEY

1 Peter 4:6

For to this end was the Gospel preached—Ever since it was given to Adam: *to them that are now dead*—In their several generations, *that they might be judged*—That though they were judged in the flesh according to the manner *of men*—With rash unrighteous judgment, they might live according to the will and word of *God in the Spirit*; the soul renewed after His image. (ENNT)

Prepare Yourself for Prayer (1 Pet. 4:7)

As Peter continued, he gave us a warning and wake-up call. He understood better than anyone how to handle suffering because he was an eyewitness to the Master's handling of crisis situations. Perhaps Peter was remembering his own failure in contrast to Jesus' total obedience to complete His work according to the Father's plan.

The end of all things is near (v. 7). Living with an attitude that the end is just around the corner brings with it an expectancy and anticipation. As we look at Jesus that day before His death, we see that His knowing the end was near gave Him a determination and a sense of urgency. It motivated Him to make sure that all was done exactly as the Father had planned it.

Peter gave us two instructions as to how we might be able to do this. The first is to be **clear minded** (v. 7). This word is elsewhere translated *serious* or *sober.* Clear-minded people are serious about their relationship with God. They keep everything in perspective.

God is calling us to be a people of wisdom. Having faith does not mean that we fail to make mature decisions based on clear reasoning. Clear-minded people do not let others influence their decisions, but are led by the wisdom of God. They are focused and have a true sense of God's purpose and direction for their lives and are not willing to cave in under duress.

We are also called to be **self-controlled** (v. 7). The self-controlled person is one who knows what he or she wants to do and then does it. Being self-controlled doesn't mean we force ourselves to do things we do not desire to do. It means that we settle the matter of our walk with God as being priority and then follow through with behavior that reflects that decision.

These two traits are necessary **so that you can pray** (v. 7). Peter remembered his own failure in this area when Jesus asked His disciples to sit and watch with Him just before His arrest (Matt. 26:36–46). Three times they tried, and three times they failed because they were not clear minded and self-controlled. Jesus knew what they wanted to do in their hearts, yet were unable to make it reality. He told them that the "spirit is willing, but the body is weak" (Matt. 26:41). If we are to cope with suffering, prayer must be at the core of our existence. This communication with the Father will keep us focused through suffering and give us the strength to endure.

Love without Exception (1 Pet. 4:8)

It is not surprising that Peter began his "grace list" with the foremost ingredient in any successful relationship—love. **Above all, love each other deeply** (v. 8). The love Peter is discussing is not an emotion, but a consistent decision leading to action. The love of Christ is real, practical, and demonstrated in our relationships. The term **deeply** means "fervently" and "without ceasing." It brings a sense of reaching out, reaching forward, and going the extra mile.

The love of Christ is the evidence of a true Christian. It has the power to transform any relationship because it **covers over a multitude of sins** (v. 8). Peter was not saying that love condones sin, but that love affirms the sinner. Paul said that love "always protects, always trusts, always hopes, always perseveres" (1 Cor. 13:7). Love empowers us to forgive. Love equips us to give the other person a break instead of harboring resentment and hostility. The unceasing love of Christ will reach the unbeliever, especially in the context of suffering.

WORDS FROM WESLEY
1 Peter 4:8

Love covereth a multitude of sins—Yea, love covereth all things. He that loves another, covereth his faults, how many soever they be. He turns away his own eyes from them; and, as for as is possible, hides them from others. And he continually prays, that all the sinner's iniquities may be forgiven and his sins covered. Meantime the God of love measures to him with the same measure into His bosom. (ENNT)

Be Hospitable (1 Pet. 4:9)

Another way God's love is seen practically is by offering **hospitality to one another without grumbling** (v. 9). Hospitality was important to the early church because there were no decent hotels.

Holiday Inn or Motel 6 didn't exist, so opening up your home to a brother or sister traveling was a simple way of expressing the love of Christ.

Today, hospitality is just as important. The home is the center-piece of your existence. It is your haven and a reflection of who you are. When you open your home, you are opening up yourself. Lasting relationships are built when you become intimate. Intimacy is built when you take what you have and offer it to another.

One of the best ways we can reach people for Christ is to invite them to see us in our home environment. This puts our commitment to Christ in proper perspective and gives the non-believer a feel for who we really are.

Being hospitable to believers shows we are willing to be vulnerable and transparent. This often leads to deeper relationships and accountability with other Christians.

Yet hospitality is not a demonstration of God's love when we complain about our guests, how they act, or how long they stay. Grumbling is a sure way to rob yourself of a blessing and extinguish the flame of God's love from your heart.

Be a Grace-Giver (1 Pet. 4:10–11)

Each one should use whatever gift he has received to serve others (v. 10). Every Christian has been given gifts by God. These gifts are God's enablement. They are the manifestation of the Spirit in that individual. These gifts are not given to hoard, but to be used.

In so many Christian churches, we have the idea that there is only one who is the minister. Yet Scripture supports the idea that all of us are ministers and therefore should be involved in ministry. The Lord knows that only in serving do we find our true fulfillment in life. So He gives us an expression of himself that we are able to give away to others. And in doing so we are **administering God's grace in its various forms** (v. 10).

A simple definition of grace is "God's unmerited favor." But as we study the Scriptures, we find that **grace** is an all-encompassing word. It refers to all God is and wants to give to us. It is His blessing, His favor, and His empowerment. God's grace is like a finely cut diamond with so many facets that we cannot number them. The term **various forms** actually means "variegated." Individually we have only a part of the whole picture, but collectively we can admire the beauty of the many aspects of His grace.

It is interesting to note that in the Greek, the word for *grace* (*charis*) is the root for the word *gift* (*charisma*). So the spiritual gifts God gives us are simply the manifestation of His grace in us. We become a channel for His use as we employ these gifts. Elsewhere in Scripture we find lists of the many gifts given by God (Rom. 12:3–8; 1 Cor. 12:7–11; Eph. 4:11–13). Each list is different. Peter, however, has reduced all these lists to two simple gifts — speaking and serving.

If anyone speaks, he should do it as one speaking the very words of God (v. 11). In other words, if we have a speaking gift, such as teaching, preaching, or encouragement, we must take heed to allow God's grace to be applied to our words. We must speak as if God is speaking through us.

One of the easiest ways to sin is with our words. We can lie, exaggerate, and deceive simply by a twist of words. So our speech impacts our ministry. James tells us that the tongue is a powerful instrument (James 3:1–10). Teachers and preachers must especially be careful not to add human opinion to God's words. Let's weigh our words before they leave our mouth!

If anyone serves, he should do it with the strength God provides (v. 11). The second gift Peter mentioned is the gift of serving. This has a myriad of applications from stuffing bulletins to visiting the sick, organizing a mission trip, or cleaning the church. The act of serving must be done in God's strength and not our own. Because serving can be such a practical gift, we sometimes forget that even the most menial task should not be completed in our own power but by God's Spirit. Otherwise we minister from a spirit of pride and not from a dependence on God. Then our gift is not the outpouring of God's grace but of our ability.

Give God the Glory (1 Pet. 4:11)

Only when we are ministering God's grace will He receive the glory. **So that in all things God may be praised through Jesus Christ** (v. 11). The gifts of God are not given to glorify us but to glorify Him. Too many have begun to assume ownership of their gifts. Too many have begun to build memorials to their ministries. God empowers us for service so that together we may manifest His glory and testify of the reality of our Savior, Jesus Christ.

The word for *grace* is also found in the Greek term *eucharistia*, which means "thanksgiving." When we truly minister God's grace to others, they in turn will praise and thank the One we serve. **To him be the glory and the power for ever and ever. Amen** (v. 11).

DISCUSSION

Christians are called to be lights in the darkness of our neighborhoods and community. Peter challenged his readers to live out their faith in a way that reflects love for God and others.

1. Peter wrote to a Christian community that had been slandered and persecuted. How did he tell them to respond?

2. How can blessing come out of suffering? When have you seen that occur?

3. In what ways do you see the name of Christ insulted today? How might a Christian bless those who do so, as Peter advised?

4. Fist Peter 4:11 admonishes Christians to pursue peace. One commentator calls it "waging peace." What are the "weapons" for "waging peace"?

5. Peter told Christians who are facing persecution and death not to fear what the world fears. What is the world afraid of? Why wouldn't Christians fear those same things?

6. The typical response to being insulted is to become angry or defensive. What might allow you to remain calm if your faith was insulted?

7. In North America, Christians are more likely to wield power than to be persecuted. What lessons-in-reverse can we draw from Peter's teaching about the right use of authority?

PRAYER

O God of our salvation, let us truly be light in a dark and dingy world. Let people look upon us to see the difference You can make in the lives of those who trust in You. May we truly set apart Jesus as Lord in our hearts and allow Him to set us apart as holy in this world.

UNEXPECTED JOY

1 Peter 4:12–19

We suffer with Christ when we faithfully endure persecution.

Most Christians living in North America do not suffer persecution. While we may experience suffering due to things such as illness, crime, or catastrophe, we are generally not singled out for ill treatment or execution because we are followers of Jesus Christ. But many people living elsewhere today are persecuted for Christ's sake.

Persecution did not fade from the Christian scene in the first century. Statisticians tell us that more people worldwide were slain for their faith in Jesus Christ during the twentieth century than in all the other previous centuries *combined*. Stories of Christians suffering for the sake of Christ still pour from places such as Asia and Africa. And while it may fall short of the suffering endured by those courageous Christians, some in our society are ridiculed or excluded by their peers for their Christian standard of moral and ethical behavior. Though we now enjoy religious freedom in the West, surveying the current global situation must cause us to ask, "Could we ever be persecuted because we follow Christ?"

In this study, Peter urged all believers to keep the faith, even while facing persecution. Don't lose hope, he says, for faithfully enduring persecution for Christ gives us a special identity with Him that comes in no other way.

COMMENTARY

Although this study begins in the middle of 1 Peter 4, many scholars believe that verse 12 is actually the beginning of a new section of this epistle. You will note (1) that verse 11 ends with "Amen," which indicates the end of a thought; and (2) that verse 12 begins with "Dear friends." First Peter 2:11 also begins with this phrase, which seems to be the beginning of a new thought in that context as well.

Whether or not this is the beginning of a new section, we find that Peter is continuing to speak of the attitude of believers as they face persecution in light of the coming judgment of Christ.

Don't Be Surprised (1 Pet. 4:12)

Verse 12 reads, **do not be surprised at the painful trial you are suffering, as though something strange were happening to you.** A common denominator for those serving Christ is suffering. The first-century church is no different from the contemporary church of today in respect to the expectation of suffering. Too often we believe that walking by faith in Christ Jesus should exempt us from suffering. Then we are caught off guard when trials come our way.

Yet in John 15:18–25, Jesus warned the disciples that as the world hated Him, they would also hate those who would follow Him. He warned them that persecution *will* come as a part of the Christian life. For as He was hated by those who reject truth, likewise we can also expect the same. Should we expect any better treatment than our Lord? We are His servants and therefore should expect to endure the same rejection He did.

The expectation of trials should be part of our Christian walk. If we expect that we should somehow be exonerated from all suffering, we will become a prime candidate for our enemy the Devil to tempt us to fall away. Anticipation prepares us as good soldiers in the army of God so that we will not be blindsided but ready to stand firm when troubles arise.

Peter spoke of the **painful trial** (v. 12) the believers were facing. If we would literally translate this phrase it would read "firing." It was a fiery ordeal that the believers were enduring. Being a Christian during Emperor Nero's reign was a terror Peter's hearers and readers had never before experienced. Nero was known for his capricious cruelty and had many ways of torturing God's people so that they would renounce their faith in Christ. Many before him had used crucifixion as a means of execution, but Nero employed other torturous acts, such as sewing people into animal skins and letting wild dogs tear them apart, or lighting people as torches to illuminate his evening festivals.

We may not face these kinds of tortures, but we will face suffering. These trials are simply a "firing" in our lives. This picture of refining by fire is reflective of Malachi 3:2–4, where God says He sits as a refiner and a purifier of His people. This passage tells us that He will refine us like silver or gold. The refining of these precious metals is a process of firing. The metal is heated until the impurities rise to the top. The refiner skims off these impurities and then reheats the metal.

How often do we feel like the heat is being turned up in our lives? What God is accomplishing is simply burning out the impurities in us that prevent us from shining for Him.

WORDS FROM WESLEY

1 Peter 4:12

Wonder not at the burning which is among you—This is the literal meaning of the expression. It seems to include both martyrdom itself, which so frequently was by fire, and all the other sufferings joined with or previous to it; *which* are permitted by the wisdom of God *for your trial*. Be not surprised at this. (ENNT)

Earlier in his letter (1 Pet. 1:6–7), Peter spoke of the faith these trials produce as being more precious than gold because the result is not only growth in our character, but also praise, glory, and honor to Christ himself. So the next time you are facing a painful trial, remember that you are in God's refining process and what He is accomplishing is much more precious than we often can understand at the moment.

Joy in the Midst of Pain (1 Pet. 4:13–14)

But rejoice that you participate in the sufferings of Christ, so that you may be overjoyed when his glory is revealed (v. 13). The idea that we should rejoice over suffering is extremely foreign to us. Suffering is something we usually grieve over, not something we rejoice about.

But Peter was not the only apostle who instructed us to rejoice in our trials. James admonished us to consider it joy when we are faced with trials (James 1:2–4). He told us that we should rejoice in our trials because they ultimately produce good in our character. Maturity comes from facing suffering by the grace of God. Suffering produces patience and perseverance—both of which are character traits of Christ himself.

WORDS FROM WESLEY

1 Peter 4:13

But as ye partake of the sufferings of Christ (ver. 1), while ye suffer for His sake, rejoice in hope of more abundant glory. For the measure of glory answers the measure of suffering; and much more abundantly. (ENNT)

Rejoicing in our suffering does not depend on our outward situation, but the inward presence of God. Joy comes from trusting Him regardless of the pain we are facing. Feeling the same rejection as He did will confirm to our hearts that we belong to Him. Conversely, we might consider that if we are not experiencing any suffering, pain, or rejection, we probably are not being effective for Christ in our area of influence.

WORDS FROM WESLEY

1 Peter 4:14

Slander'd in the cause of Jesus,
When we suffer for His name,
Jesus then delights to bless us,
Jesus dignifies our shame,
Then the Comforter is given,
Earnest of our glorious rest,
Seals the raptured heirs of heaven,
Fills His temple in our breast. (PW, vol. 13, 183)

Don't Suffer for Sin (1 Pet. 4:15)

Peter warned us, **If you suffer, it should not be as a murderer or thief or any other kind of criminal, or even as a meddler** (v. 15). Not all suffering stems from righteous acts and identification with Christ; some stems from sin.

It is important that we examine the reason for our suffering. Often we are our own worst enemy. Sin can also produce pain. Some of those who are simply bearing the consequences of their own sin are claiming martyrdom for Christ's sake.

David wrote, "Search me, O God, and know my heart; test me and know my anxious thoughts. See if there is any offensive way in me, and lead me in the way everlasting" (Ps. 139:23–24). David was not afraid to ask the Lord to turn the searchlight of the Holy Spirit into his heart to reveal the sin in his life. Likewise, we too should pray the same, that the Lord would reveal the ways we are offending and therefore causing our own painful circumstances.

Attitudes such as greed, hatred, unforgiveness, bitterness, and selfishness can all lead to suffering both in body and heart. Allowing the Lord to change us and remove these attitudes may not remove the consequences of past sins and mistakes, but as we are cleansed, we become more like Him and less likely to suffer for the wrong reasons in the future.

In other words, Peter is saying we need to know whether we are suffering for righteousness' sake or for sin. And if we are suffering for sin, we need to confess it and allow the Lord to purify our hearts from all unrighteousness (1 John 1:9).

Don't Be Ashamed (1 Pet. 4:16)

However, if you suffer as a Christian, do not be ashamed (v. 16). There is no shame in suffering for being a Christian.

The term **Christian** is a common one today, but when this letter was written it was a fairly new term. At first Christ's followers were called "believers" (Acts 1:15), "disciples" (6:1), and those "who belonged to the Way" (9:2). These followers were first called "Christians" in Antioch (Acts 11:26). The term literally means "of the household of Christ." It was a nickname used by the pagans for this new sect of Jews. King Agrippa used the term contemptuously (Acts 26:28) as he rejected Paul's testimony of Christ. The term *Christian* was a label of scorn not a badge of honor.

Today, the term is fast returning to its original context—one of disdain. Many do not understand the Christian lifestyle because of its condemnation of their own unrighteousness and have joined the ranks of those who, through the ages, have ridiculed and tormented believers who are identified as Christians.

In Acts 5:41, the apostles rejoiced because they were worthy to suffer disgrace for the name of Christ. To them this kind of rejection was a mark of God's approval on their work for His kingdom. Like the apostles, we should stand tall and not to be ashamed of being a Christian. That means we are not afraid to speak out for what is right. It means we continue to be called apart to live a godly lifestyle, rather than caving in and compromising our beliefs for the sake of being accepted.

WORDS FROM WESLEY

1 Peter 4:16

Let him glorify God—Who giveth him the honour so to suffer, and so great a reward for suffering. (ENNT)

Judgment Begins at Home (1 Pet. 4:17–18)

For it is time for judgment to begin with the family of God (v. 17). The judgment of which Peter was speaking is not judgment for our sins. Our sins were laid on Jesus, and He received the judgment for our sins at the cross. Rather, Peter was talking about the suffering that comes to the people of God.

It is interesting to note that the Old Testament prophets made mention of judgment coming to the people of God before coming to the nations (Ezek. 9:6; Zech. 13:7–9; Mal. 3:1–5). As the painful suffering of believers increases, the second coming of Christ to judge the nations cannot be far behind.

Fist Peter 4:17–18 should motivate us to have compassion on those who have not received the gospel message. It should fill us with an urgency to share the message of salvation as the time grows shorter before the coming of Messiah. Therefore, instead of nursing our emotional wounds, we should be striving even more to share our faith.

Keep on Keeping On (1 Pet. 4:19)

Peter told those who are in the midst of suffering to **commit themselves to their faithful Creator and continue to do good** (v. 19). The word **commit** reminds us of one of Christ's final words from the cross (Luke 23:26), a quotation of Psalm 31:5, often used by Jewish people as an evening prayer.

Committing ourselves to Christ means more than ensuring our entrance into heaven. It means giving all we are to God. It means knowing and trusting Him even when we are faced with the most horrific pain. Suffering should not blind our eyes to hurting people around us. Nor should it paralyze us from being effective witnesses for Christ. Rather, it should motivate us to continue to serve.

God has a plan and He knows what is best for us. Let us wholly commit ourselves to the One who created us. He knows us better than we know ourselves. Giving our pain back to Him will free us from this burden and enable us to "keep on" for Christ.

Our tendency in the midst of suffering is to lash out at those causing our pain. Yet Christ gave us an example of how to handle suffering—not with anger or hatred but with love, for love is the greatest power given us to counteract persecution. God calls us to continue to love and in doing so continue to do good as a demonstration of that love. We are being watched. How we act and react is being examined under the microscope of the unbeliever. God is testing our commitment to Him through the suffering we are experiencing. What final grade will we receive on our exam?

DISCUSSION

While not every Christian experiences persecution, it should not be a surprise if we do. Peter urged those facing persecution to respond with hope and even joy.

1. Peter told Christians not to be surprised that they are suffering. Why is surprise such a common response to suffering?

2. What does it mean that we participate in the sufferings of Christ?

3. What is the difference between suffering as a Christian and suffering for other reasons? Into which category do your sufferings usually fall?

4. Peter wrote that we are rewarded when we are "insulted because of the name of Christ" (1 Pet. 4:14). How does this compare with the teachings of other religions?

5. What do you think Peter meant by suffering "according to God's will" (v. 19)?

6. Do you think God wants you to suffer? Why?

7. What will be the result of your suffering?

8. Based on this Scripture, what advice would you give to someone who is suffering?

PRAYER

Most righteous God, we pray for Your mercy in judgment, first for believers, and then for those who do not yet believe. We pray for the salvation of the world. Give us strength to sacrifice ourselves for You just as You have sacrificed yourself for us.

THE HABIT OF HOLINESS

1 Peter 5:1–14

Humility is a distinguishing characteristic of the Christian life.

A flamboyant sports personality once made this claim: "I am the greatest boxing promoter in the world. And I say that humbly." Probably no other Christian virtue is as little understood as humility. Even when we try to be humble, we seem to fall short.

✴ Humility is having a right attitude about oneself. It is not thinking of ourselves more highly than we ought. Humility is that elusive virtue that allows us to be hard on ourselves and easier on others. Humility was perfectly modeled by Jesus Christ, and His humility is summarized by the apostle Paul in Philippians 2:7: "[He] made himself nothing, taking the very nature of a servant." And humility is one more thing—the hallmark of a holy life. This virtue is the guarantee that we will always get more of whatever holiness we already possess; only the humble are spiritually hungry.

Throughout 1 Peter, the good apostle declared that humility is the habit of holiness. He stressed the virtue of humility as a sort of glue that binds together all other virtues. This study is a clear call to follow the example of Jesus Christ and to humble yourselves so that you may become like Christ.

COMMENTARY

Although 1 Peter is only five chapters, it is brimming with allusions to the writings of Paul, James, and the Old Testament. It contains a plethora of exhortations to a church scattered throughout Asia Minor (1:1) undergoing intense persecution and suffering. Peter was doing what many of us might do if we had a friend struggling through difficult circumstances: write a letter peppered with encouragement from Scripture. We might not cite chapter and verse, but we would certainly depend more on God's words than on our own. We would offer every bit of helpful advice we could think of, not necessarily going into great detail, but offering nuggets of truth to refresh and motivate. And so it is with Peter.

Expectation of Elders (1 Pet. 5:1–4)

Peter began by addressing **the elders among you** (v. 1). Although the administrative structure of the church was not highly developed at this time, the office of elder had already been instituted (see Acts 11:30; 14:23; 20:17; 21:18). These men (generally older, but not always, as in the case of Timothy) were responsible for the spiritual leadership of the church and the care of its members. Peter addressed them first because leadership always sets the example. **I appeal as a fellow elder** (1 Pet. 5:1). Although Peter, as an apostle, had authority over these elders, he chose to identify himself with them so they would realize he was speaking as a brother who understood exactly what they were experiencing. He reminded them that he was **a witness of Christ's sufferings**, which he also specifically mentioned in Acts 3:15 and Acts 10:39. He may have mentioned this as a further attestation to his authority or simply as a reminder that Christ himself suffered on their behalf and Peter intimately understood the struggle of his readers.

In 1 Peter 4:13, he had told them to rejoice in their sufferings "that you may be overjoyed when his glory is revealed." And Peter identified with them here in 5:1, describing himself as **one who also will share in the glory to be revealed**. Peter knew what it was like to suffer. Acts 5:40 records his flogging, but it is probable that he suffered many additional trials in subsequent years.

Be shepherds of God's flock that is under your care, Peter exhorted in 1 Peter 5:2. They were to remember that the flock was God's, not theirs. Like shepherds, they were to care for, lead, guide, and protect their flock. But notice how they were to do it: **not because you must, but because you are willing** (v. 2) and **not lording it over those entrusted to you, but being examples** (v. 3). They were to avoid the trap of becoming a hired hand, simply performing their duties because it was their job. Their manner of ministry should be one of willing service, not of compulsion.

WORDS FROM WESLEY
1 Peter 5:2

What is a minister of Christ, a shepherd of souls, unless he is all devoted to God? . . . Is he not called, above others, to be an example to the flock, in his private as well as public character? An example of all holy and heavenly tempers, filling the heart so as to shine through the life? Consequently, is not his whole life, if he walks worthy of his calling, one incessant labour of love; one continued tract of praising God, and helping man; one series of thankfulness and beneficence? Is he not always humble, always serious, though rejoicing evermore; mild, gentle, patient, abstinent? May you not resemble him to a guardian angel, ministering to those "who shall be heirs of salvation?" Is he not one sent forth from God, to stand between God and man, to guard and assist the poor, helpless children of men, to supply them both with light and strength, to guide them through a thousand known and unknown dangers, till at the appointed time He returns, with those committed to his charge, to his and their Father who is in heaven?

O who is able to describe such a messenger of God, faithfully executing his high office! working together with God, with the great Author both of the old and of the new creation! (WJW, vol. 10, 487–488)

Peter also addressed the motives of the shepherds. He expected them not to be **greedy for money** (v. 2) as was often the case with itinerant teachers. It seems unlikely that the church would have been a great source of wealth at this time in its history, but greed doesn't require the prospects of a lot of money. It's simply an attitude of the heart. Peter expected them to be **eager to serve** (v. 2) for the sake of serving. Their zeal and enthusiasm were to come from the ministry itself, not from the prospect of obtaining money.

Their faithfulness to these expectations would result in a great reward: **And when the Chief Shepherd appears, you will receive the crown of gory that will never fade away** (v. 4) Jesus himself, **the Chief Shepherd** (a term used only here, but see Heb. 13:20), will give them a crown of glory when He returns. The imagery of a crown here isn't the kingly crown but the victor's crown, a wreath of amaranth flowers, which normally would wither in a short time. This crown, though, would never fade. They would receive the commendation, "Well done, good and faithful servant" (Matt. 25:21, 23), the greatest glory any of us could hope for.

Expectation of the Young (1 Pet. 5:5–9)

In verses 5–9, Peter gave practical advice to the young men in the churches (in contrast to "those who are older" and the "elders" of v. 1, both of which use the same Greek word). These **young men** (v. 5) may have held positions within the churches as associate pastors, or they may be addressed here simply because they were also expected to set an example. There can be no doubt, though, that these expectations also applied to women of all ages; they are universal.

Be submissive to those who are older (v. 5) is an important expectation. The church would never function properly if everyone led and no one followed. Those who were younger or less-experienced (or simply younger in their walk with the Lord) were to willingly place themselves under the authority of those who were leaders. It is interesting to note that the word translated **older** in the NIV is the same word for "elder" in verse 1, which may indicate that this was an admonition to submit to the elders of the church. (See 1 Thess. 5:12–13.)

Clothe yourselves with humility toward one another (1 Pet. 5:5). The word **clothe** (used only here in the New Testament) is derived from a Greek word that means "a knot or band." According to one commentator, the corresponding noun referred to an apron worn by slaves that they tied tightly around the waist to keep them clean. The close correlation of the word **clothe** with a slave indicates that the young men should be willing to assume lowly positions in the church, just as Jesus did when He girded himself with a towel (an apron) and washed the feet of the disciples (John 13:4–5). This attitude of humility is not easy to develop, **but** God **gives grace to the humble** and will enable them to meet this expectation (1 Pet. 5:5; see also Prov. 3:34).

●

WORDS FROM WESLEY

1 Peter 5:5

When our inmost soul is thoroughly tinctured therewith, it remains that we "be clothed with humility." The word used by St. Peter seems to imply that we be covered with it as with a surtout [an overcoat]; that we be all humility, both within and without; tincturing all we think, speak, and do. Let all our actions spring from this fountain; let all our words breathe this spirit; that all men may know we have been with Jesus, and have learned of Him to be lowly in heart. (WJW, vol. 6, 398)

The young men were also to **humble** themselves **under God's mighty hand** (1 Pet. 5:6). It is possible that here Peter was referring to the trials and persecutions they were enduring, which served to teach humility. Once the lesson was learned and their character had been developed, God would **lift** them **up in due time** (v. 6). God himself was not the cause of their trials, but He was certainly in control. He often allows trials to perfect His people. (See James 1:2–4; Heb. 12:10–11; Rom. 8:28.)

Cast all your anxiety on him because he cares for you (1 Pet. 5:7). Peter expected these Christians to trust God. It's understandable that they were anxious, given their suffering, but they needed to hold on to the fact that God cared for them—that He loved them more than they loved themselves, wanted to bless them more than they wanted to be blessed, wanted to provide for their needs more than they wanted to be provided for. Once we understand God's great love for us, we can't help but forget our troubles.

Be self-controlled and alert (v. 8). This matter required their instant attention, especially in the face of their suffering. Suffering can either make us better or bitter. It can mold our character or destroy us. We cannot afford to be lazy and inattentive, because our **enemy the devil prowls around like a roaring lion looking for someone to devour** (v. 8). **Enemy** is a translation of the Hebrew word for Satan. The Greek word is used of an opponent in a lawsuit (Matt. 5:25) or for an adversary. Satan is out to get us.

WORDS FROM WESLEY

1 Peter 5:8

But in the mean time *watch*. There is a close connection between this and the duly casting our care upon Him. How deeply had St. Peter himself suffered for want of watching! *Be vigilant*—As if he had said, awake and keep awake. Sleep no more, be this your care. *As a roaring lion*—Full of rage, *seeking*—With all subtlety likewise, *whom he may devour* or *swallow up*—Both soul and body. (ENNT)

We must **resist him, standing firm in the faith** (1 Pet. 5:9). James said, "Resist the devil, and he will flee from you" (James 4:7). That's right. He'll take right off once you decide to resist, once you stand on your faith and determine to trust the Lord. Contrary to popular opinion, Satan is not all-powerful. He is not all-knowing. He is not all-present. He is a limited being with limited power, and we have the power to resist him and send him running. That is great news for these suffering Christians. They need to stand firm, then, **because you know that your brothers throughout the world are undergoing the same kind of sufferings** (1 Pet. 5:9). They needed to be strong as a witness to others undergoing trials.

WORDS FROM WESLEY

1 Peter 5:10

Now the God of all grace—By which alone the whole work is began, continued, and finished in your soul: *after ye have suffered awhile*—A very little while, compared with eternity: *himself*—Ye have only to watch and resist the devil: the rest God will perform: *perfect*— That no defect may remain: *stablish*—That nothing may overthrow you: *strengthen*—That ye may conquer all adverse power: *and settle you*—As a house upon a rock. So the apostle, being converted, does now strengthen his brethren. (ENNT)

Expectation of God (1 Pet. 5:10–11)

Peter fully expected that God would be faithful. **And the God of all grace . . . after you have suffered a little while, will himself restore you and make you strong, firm and steadfast** (v. 10). The word **while** doesn't appear in the Greek text, so Peter might actually have been referring to intensity, not time. They are really only suffering a little in comparison to what Christ had suffered for them. And their suffering is quite short-lived, because God is gracious. He will **restore** them, a reference to finishing, completing, or repairing. God will repair us and bring to completion what is lacking in our character. He has **called you to his eternal glory in Christ** (v. 10), and we can be assured that He will deliver on His promises. Peter ended with a doxology: **To him be the power for ever and ever.**

Amen (v. 11; see 4:11), a reminder to his readers that God is the one who is ultimately in control. He is the all-powerful one, not the Enemy.

Concluding Remarks (1 Pet. 5:12–14)

Peter mentioned that he wrote this letter **with the help of Silas** (v. 12). This is the same Silas mentioned in Acts 15–18; 2 Corinthians 1:19; and 1 Thessalonians 1:1. He was a trusted companion of Paul. Since the Greek of 1 Peter is so much more polished than the rough Greek of 2 Peter, many have assumed from this verse that Silas here acted as Peter's secretary.

In any case, Peter wrote this letter for the purpose of **encouraging you and testifying that this is the true grace of God** (1 Pet. 5:12). In Luke 22:32, Jesus had told Peter, "But I have prayed for you, Simon, that your faith may not fail. And when you have turned back, strengthen your brothers." And that is exactly what Peter set out to do in this short letter. He testified to the truth of the grace that God offers in times of suffering. Now his readers must **stand fast in it** (1 Pet. 5:12). He knew that "God's solid foundation stands firm" (2 Tim. 2:19) and exhorted them to hold fast to it.

Two interesting questions are in 1 Peter 5:13. **She who is in Babylon, chosen together with you, sends you her greetings**. The first question is who is **she**? Some believe Peter was speaking of the church from which he was writing. But because he also mentioned **so does my son Mark**, the logical assumption is that he was speaking of a particular person. Because he didn't mention her name, it was probably someone already known to the recipients of this message.

Peter asked them to **Greet one another with a kiss of love** (v. 14). This was the custom of the day, equivalent to our modern-day hug or handshake. The final benediction comes at the end of verse 14: **Peace to all of you who are in Christ.** When we are **in Christ**, in a personal relationship with Him, there is peace even in the midst of the storm. Jesus said, "In this world you will have trouble. But take heart! I have overcome the world" (John 16:33).

DISCUSSION

The way of the world is to seek attention for one's own sake. But the way of Christ is to exercise genuine humility—to make oneself "nothing" in order to serve God and others.

1. Why do you think some people lord their leadership over others?

2. What are the rewards mentioned for faithful leaders? What examples have you seen of faithful leaders in the church? In what ways were they examples to others?

3. To exercise leadership requires having vision and a desire to see things accomplished. Yet humility is listed as a key characteristic of a good leader. How is it possible for a leader to be both ambitious and humble?

4. What are the things that cause the most stress in our society? In you? In what practical ways can we cast all of our anxieties on Christ?

5. Peter pictured the Enemy as a roaring lion, seeking to devour us. In what ways does the enemy attack us? How can we be prepared to deal with those attacks?

6. What habits or activities support you in developing self-control and in standing firm when tempted? What habits or activities detract from your ability to resist?

PRAYER

Most Holy God, grant us a spirit of humility that will strengthen us against the wiles of the Devil. Help us to remain connected to the vine, Christ Jesus and His church, that we may not become separated from the flock and devoured by that prowling lion.

9

HOW TO BECOME A CONFIDENT CHRISTIAN

2 Peter 1:1–11

A Christian displays godly qualities in ever-increasing measure.

Is it possible to know for sure that we are God's children? Peter's answer to that question is a simple yes. Through Jesus Christ, God has provided all that we need to know Him, find salvation, and live a godly life that is pleasing in His sight. We can have complete assurance that we are headed for eternity with Him.

This study provides a boost of confidence for Christians who may be struggling with doubt or defeat. While the doubts and temptations may continue to assault us, Peter wanted us to feel certain that our faith is secure and our future with Christ is assured. How is this possible? It is because we know Christ and have tied our lives to His.

COMMENTARY

New Testament Epistles followed this well-known pattern. First came the writer's name and possibly a self-description; then the recipient was identified. The writer sent greetings, usually gave a word of thanksgiving, and then proceeded to the main body of the letter. The closing of the letter might include personal greetings, a closing charge, and a benediction. Most of these elements are included here in 2 Peter. It is important to pay close attention to these details because often a writer will give important hints about the overall purpose of the letter in these seemingly mundane details.

Introduction and Greeting (2 Pet. 1:1–2)

Simon Peter, a servant and apostle of Jesus Christ (v. 1). Double names were common in the ancient world. A person had a birth name in his or her language and a Greek name because it was the common language in the Roman Empire. Here the combination includes both his given Hebrew and Greek name. He also identified himself as **a servant and apostle of Jesus Christ**. The term communicates humility, but it was also used to designate great leaders of the past, such as Moses (Heb. 3:5; Rev. 15:3) or David (Luke 1:69; Acts 4:25). An **apostle** (2 Pet. 1:1) was someone especially chosen by Christ to be His witness and ambassador. Thus, Peter stressed both his obedience to Christ and that he was chosen as a disciple.

The recipients of this letter were not in one locale like Rome or Corinth, but were connected **through the righteousness of our God and Savior Jesus Christ** (v. 1). This is one of the few times in the New Testament where Jesus is explicitly called **God**. It is His righteousness that is the common bond between believers. Peter spoke of their **faith as precious as ours**, affirming the equal status of both Jews and Gentiles in the new covenant community.

Following the identification of the writer and recipient comes the greeting: **Grace and peace** (v. 2) were the standard part of the greeting, but what is fascinating here is how this comes about: **through the knowledge of God and of Jesus our Lord.** This introduces one of the key ideas throughout the epistle: knowledge. It is mentioned in each of the next two paragraphs. In fact, the book begins and ends with an important reference to knowledge (see 3:18). This knowledge is not just an acquaintance with facts, but a knowledge that changes.

The Source of Spiritual Growth (2 Pet. 1:3–4)

Most Epistles follow the greeting with a word of thanksgiving (see Rom. 1:8; 1 Cor. 1:4; Phil. 1:3). This epistle instead launches right into the body of the letter. In chapter 2, the problem of false teachers will be addressed. Chapter 1 presents the positive picture of what should be taking place in the life of every Christian—spiritual growth. This is the first defense against false teaching.

Before we get to the how of spiritual growth, we must recognize the source: **His divine power . . . who called us by his own glory and goodness** (2 Pet. 1:3). All true spiritual growth comes from God. God not only is the source, but He generously **has given us everything we need for life and godliness** (v. 3). The means is also clear: **through our knowledge of him who called us** (v. 3). It is emphasized that this **knowledge** is active with specific content. The content consists of **his very great and precious promises** (v. 4). The active is also emphasized: **so that through them you may participate in the divine nature and escape the corruption in the world caused by evil desires** (v. 4).

Peter used some startling words for both his day and ours. For example, **divine nature** (v. 4), **godliness**, and **goodness** (v. 3) were pagan terms very common in the first-century culture. In our day, a phrase like **participate in the divine nature** (v. 4) may remind us of some so-called New Age jargon. In fact, the specific terms Peter used here are relatively rare in the New Testament. In so doing, he would use some of the keys words of the false teachers against them and reveal the truth about the relationship between God and people. Both **godliness** and **goodness** (v. 3) were common words connected to ethical behavior.

The Pursuit of Spiritual Growth (2 Pet. 1:5–9)

As we have just seen, God has promised through grace a means of "escape [from] the corruption in the world" (1:4). This does not mean that it happens automatically, simply by an act of God. He has not chosen to work this way. Instead, Peter exhorted us, **make every effort to add to your faith** (v. 5). One contemporary way to restate Peter's admonition is "spare no expense."

The original word behind **add** comes from an ancient Greek practice where wealthy patrons sponsored the choruses in a play, often competing for the most extravagant production. The word developed the meaning of "generous and costly cooperation," which is the way it is used here.

WORDS FROM WESLEY

2 Peter 1:5

For this very reason—Because God hath given you so great blessings *giving all diligence*—It is a very uncommon word, which we render *giving*. It literally signifies, *bringing in by the by*, or *over and above*; implying, that God works the work; yet not unless we are diligent. Our diligence is to follow the gift of God, and is followed by an increase of all His gifts; *add to*—And *in* all the other gifts of God. Superadd the latter, without losing the former. The Greek word properly means *lead up*, as in a dance, one of these after the other, in a beautiful order. *Your faith*, that *evidence of things not seen*, termed before *the knowledge of God and of Christ*—The root of all Christian graces; *courage*—Whereby ye may conquer all enemies and difficulties, and execute whatever faith dictates. In this most beautiful connection, each preceding grace leads to the following: each following, tempers and perfects the preceding. They are set down in the order of nature, rather than the order of time. For though every grace bears a relation to every other, yet here they are so nicely ranged, that those which have the closest dependence on each other, are placed together; *and to your courage knowledge*—Wisdom, teaching how to exercise it on all occasions. (ENNT)

Faith (v. 5) is the first in a list of qualities that culminates with **love** (v. 7). Most of the items in the list are similar to the types of lists compiled by first-century moralists. There is a great deal of overlap between what the world recognized as the best moral qualities and what Peter listed here. It can be argued that this is a reflection of common grace, because God is the Creator of all of us. This does not mean that two such lists will always be identical, but it should not surprise us to see a great deal of overlap.

This list, however, begins and ends with characteristic Christian qualities. (See 2 Cor. 8:7 for another list that begins and ends this way.)

The starting point for any Christian is **faith** (2 Pet. 1:5). God calls, we respond in faith, and then we must act. James 2:26 concludes bluntly, "Faith without deeds is dead." Paul explained the divine and human aspects this way: "Continue to work out your salvation with fear and trembling, for it is God who works in you to will and to act according to his good purpose" (Phil. 2:12–13). Becoming the kind of person God wants is a cooperative effort.

The next item to add is **goodness** (2 Pet. 1:5). The original word, *arête*, is quite rare in the New Testament, but common in Greek thought to designate "excellence" or "proper fulfillment of anything." For example, a good knife cuts well or a horse must run. Christians must fulfill the purpose God has for them.

Following **goodness** is **knowledge** (v. 5), which is a key theme of the epistle. In non-Christian lists this quality is usually first or last. This attribute helps a person see the true issues, make right choices, and live wisely. It is the practical application of the intellect. Some false teachers argued that once a person knew the "truth," further actions were either unnecessary or irrelevant. Some teachers, so-called Gnostics, insisted that actions made no difference to a person's standing before God. To them the next quality is a stinging rebuke: add to **knowledge, self-control** (v. 6). Knowing truth is not a license for immoral behavior, but should be accompanied by the ability to take a grip of oneself. The only other list that uses **self-control** in the New Testament contrasts it with "the acts of the sinful nature" (Gal. 5:19–23).

Perseverance (2 Pet. 1:6) is a steady endurance in the face of difficulty. The root of the original word is a combination of "under" and "remain." It is not a simple passive acceptance, but the determination to be faithful and trust in God while waiting for the fulfillment of His promises. The writer of Hebrews tells us, "Do not throw away your confidence; it will be richly rewarded. You need to persevere so that when you have done the will of God, you will receive what he has promised" (10:34–35).

Godliness (2 Pet. 1:6) was a very important ethical term for the Greeks. The term literally meant "good worship." The great philosopher Aristotle said it had three parts: duty to one's gods, to one's dead ancestors, and to family and parents. To use Christian terminology, it is the proper respect for the vertical dimensions in a person's life, both toward God and those human beings who have authority over us.

The New Testament writers frequently refer to fellow Christians in terms of kinship, most commonly brothers. As the early church expanded, even their enemies commented on the **brotherly kindness** (v. 7) among Christians. Like any family, this did not mean that the Christians never had disagreements, but something more fundamental bound them together—a recognition of their heavenly Father.

The culmination of the list is **love** (v. 7). This is of course *agape* love—a love that results from a choice to desire the best for another person. It is not earned. This list is subject to two misunderstandings. A person could look at this list and be overwhelmed and become discouraged over attaining any of the qualities. A second mistake sees the qualities as a progression where one must be mastered before moving on to the next. Both of these misunderstandings are addressed in the next verse: **For if you possess these qualities in increasing measure, they will keep you from being ineffective and unproductive in your knowledge of our Lord Jesus Christ** (v. 8). Notice the word **increasing**. We already have "everything we need" (v. 3), and now we must keep moving in the right direction.

WORDS FROM WESLEY
2 Peter 1:8

For these being really *in you*—Added to your faith, *and abounding*—Increasing more and more, otherwise we fall short, *make you neither slothful nor unfruitful*—Do not suffer you to be faint in your mind, or without fruit in your lives. If there is less faithfulness, less care and watchfulness, since we were pardoned, than there were before, and less diligence, less outward obedience, than when we were seeking remission of sin, we are both *slothful and unfruitful in the knowledge of Christ*—That is, in the faith, which then cannot work by love. (ENNT)

The last verse contrasts the person in whom these qualities are lacking: **he is nearsighted and blind, and has forgotten that he has been cleansed from his past sins** (v. 8). The NIV reverses the order of **nearsighted** and **blind** probably to communicate the idea of increasing severity. The question remains why the original has the order "blind and nearsighted." This is the only occurrence of **nearsighted** in the New Testament. It means "to blink" or "shut the eyes." One possible reason for the original order is that the term includes the idea of willfulness. The blind person cannot see because the ability is missing, but some people fail to see because they close their eyes and refuse to look.

The Urgency of Spiritual Growth (2 Pet. 1:10–11)

The promise of being effective and productive and the warning of willful blindness is the motive for being **all the more eager to make your calling and election sure** (v. 10). Again we have the combination of faith and works. God is the one who calls and elects, but we must respond.

The Christian who eagerly desires to grow and acts on that desire "will never come to grief" (v. 10 NEB). It is not meant as a foolproof guarantee of entry into heaven, but of staying in step with what God wants. It is doing the will of God that will ensure **a rich welcome into the eternal kingdom of our Lord and Savior Jesus Christ** (v. 11). Salvation begins with the call of God and culminates in eternity with God. Between now and then, God gives us the opportunity and responsibility to ready ourselves.

WORDS FROM WESLEY

2 Peter 1:10

How shall I make my calling sure?
By penitence and faith in Thee
(Whose death my pardon did procure
And bought eternal life for me).
By wrestling on in instant prayer,
By listening to the gospel-word,
Till Thou Thy saving name declare,
And faith beholds its bleeding Lord.
Soon as the blood has touch'd my heart
I my effectual calling know,
From all iniquity depart,
And in Thy shining footsteps go;
Walking in Thee, I go in peace
Thine acceptable will to prove,
And follow after holiness,
True holiness, and perfect love. (PW, vol. 13, 190)

DISCUSSION

While we might hope for instantaneous transformation, the New Testament describes a lifelong pathway that leads to a godly, mature, virtuous life.

1. Peter said that God's divine power has given us everything we need for life and godliness. What are these things we need?

2. How can we tap into God's power and have access to those things?

3. What do you think it means to participate in the divine nature? How would we do that?

4. Peter provided building blocks of godly characteristics that seem to build on each other. Read the list and describe how each of these virtues builds on the previous one (2 Pet. 1:5–7).

5. Peter urged us to take action by adding these virtues to our lives. Yet we often try and fail to be more godly. What's missing?

6. According to Peter, some believers don't go on to add these virtues to their lives. How did he describe them? What examples of this have you seen?

7. What do you think it means to make our calling and election sure? Do you think there is some doubt about whether or not we are saved?

8. How well does your church or small group do at supporting people in becoming more mature in the ways described in this Scripture? What would increase its effectiveness?

PRAYER

O most generous God, give us the fortitude and determination to possess your qualities in an ever increasing measure, that we may be productive in Your service.

THE AUTHORITY OF SCRIPTURE

2 Peter 1:12–21

The Bible is our infallible guide for life and faith.

How do you know for sure that the things you believe are true? What makes the Bible different from the Quran any other religious writing? In an age when many believe that scientific discoveries hold the answers to life's ultimate questions, why should we continue to rely on an ancient book as the source of truth?

People have always had questions about the value of Scripture, as Peter knew when writing to early believers in Asia Minor. One aim of his writing was to inform them of reasons why the Bible is trustworthy and should be given a place of authority in their lives. This isn't simply a book; it is God's book. Though written over hundreds of years by many writers, each was inspired by God to record the history, song, prophecy, sermon, or letter that is now comprised in the sixty-six books of the Bible.

How do we know the Bible is somehow different? We know God's Word is real because it works—it continually guides, rebukes, informs, encourages, and corrects believers no matter where or when they live. This study will take you deeper into this powerful writing called Scripture and give you a greater love and passion for the written Word of God.

COMMENTARY

Before turning to the specific charges against false teachers in chapter 2, Peter wanted to firmly reinforce the truth. A common illustration asserts that the best way to identify counterfeit money is a very thorough knowledge and experience of the genuine. When you know the real, the imperfections of the false are easily recognized.

Remembering the Truth (2 Pet. 1:12–15)

Peter made the transition to this paragraph by introducing it with the words: **So I will always remind you of these things** (v. 12). What is said here cannot be viewed in isolation but continues his words about growth from the previous section. He was not introducing new information, but reiterating what the readers already knew. One of the most important functions of the Christian ministry is to remind people of truth already known. Memory is a very important element in spiritual growth. Israelite parents were exhorted to teach their children both God's commandments and past actions (Deut. 6:4–12). They also built monuments or reenacted the great acts of God. In Joshua's day, they built a monument when God helped them cross the Jordan (Josh. 4:19–24). Another monument reminded them of the covenant requirements (Josh. 24:26–27). Several of the yearly feasts were memorials. The best-known is the Passover, which celebrated deliverance from Egypt. In the New Testament, Jesus instituted the Lord's Supper as a permanent reminder of His sacrifice for us.

Reminders are not just for new Christians. Peter wrote, **even though you know them and are firmly established in the truth you now have. I think it is right to refresh your memory as long as I live** (2 Pet. 1:12–13). We need to be reminded of the profound truths of the gospel. This does not necessarily lead to dull repetition; the same truths can be conveyed in many different ways. The danger is that in searching for novel ways and methods to communicate, the central message may be lost. As one business consultant put it, "The main thing is to the keep the main thing the main thing."

A special urgency motivates the writing of this letter. Peter knew that his life was just about finished. Some scholars see this epistle as his last will and testament. To confirm that Peter thought these were his final words, it is alluded to at least three times within this paragraph. It is implied by **as long as I live in the tent of this body** (v. 13), confirmed by **because I know that I will soon put it aside** (v. 14), and reiterated by **I will make every effort to see that after my departure you will always be able to remember these things** (v. 15).

Two interesting connected words in this paragraph are **tent** (v. 13) and **departure** (v. 15). The patriarchs lived in tents. The same root word is used by John to speak of Jesus coming into the world: "The Word became flesh and made his *dwelling* among us" (John 1:14, emphasis added). It is a reminder that this world is not permanent just as a tent is not a permanent structure. The Greek word behind **departure** (2 Pet. 1:15) is "exodus." Peter's coming death would indeed be a journey to the Promised Land! Most scholars think that the comment about the timing of Peter's death is a reference to Jesus' words in John 21:18: "I tell you the truth, when you were younger you dressed yourself and went where you wanted; but when you are old you will stretch out your hands, and someone else will dress you and lead you where you do not want to go."

WORDS FROM WESLEY
2 Peter 1:14

In this tabernacle—Or *tent*. How short is our abode in the body! How easily does a believer pass out of it! (ENNT)

Apostles Attest the Truth (2 Pet. 1:16–18)

Peter's desire that we remember his teachings is fulfilled as we read and follow his words as they have been handed down to us.

He also wants to make it very clear that the message he proclaimed was not just his private individual opinion. The singular *I* of the previous paragraph shifts to the plural *we* to signify the testimony of all the apostles. The message is not a new one, but one the readers had already received.

The first sentence makes a very important contrast between **cleverly invented stories** and **eyewitnesses** (v. 16). The original word for **stories** is *mythos*. *Myth* had at least two different meanings when Peter wrote, just as it does today. To many ancient Greeks the term applied to stories about the interaction of their ancient heroes and gods. Most did not believe them as reports of literal events, but narratives that communicated moral or philosophical truths. The actions of the characters illustrated important lessons for humans. Teachers used the stories as allegories. To other Greeks, all myths were treated with contempt, complete nonsense suitable only for young children.

Peter was not just passing on what he heard about Jesus. He asserted that he was a member of the apostles who **were eyewitnesses of his majesty** (v. 16). The word **eyewitness**, which occurs only here in the New Testament, is one that carries with it more than just being a spectator, but one who was involved in what was described. Not only did Peter see, he also **heard** God's **voice that came from heaven** (v. 18). From the place mentioned and words quoted, it is clear that Peter was referring to the transfiguration. He used this incident not as a glimpse of the resurrection of Jesus, but as a picture of the second coming, or *parousia*.

One proof of the truth of the gospel of Jesus is the testimony of the apostles. However, their experiences did not happen in isolation. Peter affirmed that the prophets prepared the way. They too testify to the validity of the Christian message.

Prophets Reveal the Truth (2 Pet. 1:19–21)

The ministry of Jesus Christ was not a chance event. At the transfiguration, two significant people from the Old Testament appeared with Jesus: Moses and Elijah. These individuals serve as representatives for the Law and the Prophets. God used Moses to deliver the law to the ancient Israelites. Elijah set the pattern for the many prophets that followed as he reminded the Israelites that they were to be devoted to God alone. The Law and the Prophets, which is the usual New Testament title for the Old Testament, set the stage for Jesus. For those who were paying attention, the coming of Jesus was the fulfillment of an old message. However, the earthly ministry of Christ did not exhaust all that the prophets said about the coming Messiah. Some of their words have still to be fulfilled. Yet given how many of them have been fulfilled, we can have confidence in the rest of their message. This seems to be the thought behind Peter's statement that **we have the word of the prophets made more certain** (v. 19). The prophetic word must still be heeded as **a light shining in a dark place** because it reveals where we are and also where we are going. This will continue **until the day dawns and the morning star rises in your hearts** (v. 19). **Morning star** is literally "light-bringer," an obvious reference to Jesus (see Rev. 22:16). The day that Peter was referring to is not the first coming of Christ, because he stated that **you will do well to pay attention** to the words of the prophets (2 Pet. 1:19). Many Christians seem to forget that the Old Testament it still important for us. We ignore it to our peril.

The prophets' words are trustworthy because they do not reflect merely the thoughts of the prophets. Verses 20–21 are very important for understanding the inspired nature of Scripture. We must be careful to see not only what this passage does say, but also what it does not. Understanding the pagan notion of prophetic inspiration also makes an informative contrast.

WORDS FROM WESLEY

2 Peter 1:19

Nor is this profitable only for the men of God, for those who walk already in the light of his countenance; but also for those who are yet in darkness, seeking him whom they know not. Thus St. Peter, "We have also a more sure word of prophecy:" Literally, "And we have the prophetic word more sure" . . . confirmed by our being "eye-witnesses of his Majesty," and "hearing the voice which came from the excellent glory"; unto which—prophetic word; so he styles the Holy Scriptures—"ye do well that ye take heed, as unto a light that shineth in a dark place, until the day dawn, and the Day-star arise in your hearts" (2 Pet. 1:19). Let all, therefore, who desire that day to dawn upon their hearts, wait for it in searching the Scriptures. (WJW, vol. 5, 194)

Pagan Greek prophecy was quite different from the Old Testament. A person seeking to know the will of the gods would travel to a place where the gods spoke, the Oracle of Delphi. The Greeks believed that the mountain on which it was located was the middle of the earth. The process of communication was as follows: The god who wished to speak possessed a mantis (we get the word *mania* from the same root) who often fell into an ecstatic trance before speaking. The words were often obscure and vague and needed to be interpreted by another intermediary, who might put the oracle into poetry or even write it down for the seeker. How different were the ancient Hebrew prophets! They spoke directly and clearly to their listeners. This does not mean that everything they said was simple, but there was little doubt from their words what God wanted of the people.

●

WORDS FROM WESLEY

WORDS FROM WESLEY
2 Peter 1:20

Ye do well, *as knowing this, that no Scripture prophecy is of private interpretation.* It is not any man's own word. It is God, not the prophet himself, who thereby interprets things till then unknown. (ENNT)

As mentioned earlier, Peter provided two proofs of the gospel message: the eyewitness testimony of the apostles and the words of the prophets. Together these testimonies reinforce each other. The prophets were not direct eyewitnesses to the accomplishments of Jesus, but "they only saw them and welcomed them from a distance" (Heb. 11:13). They did not speak "cleverly invented stories" (2 Pet. 1:16). Nor did they simply look at their situation and state their own analysis of what would happen. **No prophecy of Scripture came about by the prophet's own interpretation** (v. 20). Nor were their words some kind of hopeful wish, but **men spoke from God as they were carried along by the Holy Spirit** (v. 21). The picture behind **carried along** is a ship with raised sails pushed along by the wind (see Acts 27:15–17). Unlike the Greek mantis, the Hebrew prophets were not mere passive objects who mumbled incomprehensibly, but passionate proclaimers of what they received.

Some have understood the doctrine of the inspiration of Scripture as a dictation. This understanding is more or less what Muslims believe: Allah dictated the Quran to Muhammad. The Christian doctrine of inspiration is *not* dictation. Notice again the phrase **men spoke from God** (2 Pet. 1:21). A quick survey of the Old Testament prophets reveals that each spoke in his own vocabulary and style. For example, Isaiah told very little about himself, while Jeremiah included several of his personal complaints about the way he was treated. Haggai gave very precise dates to his messages, while the exact time when Joel ministered is still highly debated. Amos is written mostly in poetry, while Daniel used mostly prose. Ezekiel received majestic visions of God and a restored temple, while Malachi used a simple question-and-answer format. It is quite clear that the personalities of the prophets were not submerged, but are reflected in what they recorded. However, the prophets were not spouting their own opinion. God spoke through them without subverting their personalities. If someone asks, "Are the words of the Bible divine or human?" The correct answer is "both." It is the Word of God in the words of people. Denying either one distorts the true nature of Scripture.

WORDS FROM WESLEY
2 Peter 1:21

For prophecy came not of old by the will of man—Of any mere man whatever, *but the holy men of God*—Devoted to Him, and set apart by Him for that purpose, *spake*, and wrote, *being moved*—Literally carried. They were purely passive therein. (ENNT)

DISCUSSION

Peter was clear about the reason why the Scriptures have authority—because they do not reflect the opinions or interpretations of humans, but the voice of God.

1. Peter wanted to be sure his loved ones remembered what was important to him. What things was he talking about? What was he doing to preserve that legacy?

2. Peter was an eyewitness to the resurrection of Jesus. He took pains to point that out to his readers. Why would he do so?

3. What objections to the gospel do people raise today?

4. Following Peter's example here, how can we make our case for the validity of the gospel message? What's our evidence or what is the basis for our claims?

5. In what way do the words of the prophets verify Peter's testimony?

6. Do you think people today are more impressed by historical evidence, scientific proof, or personal testimony?

7. What is the best evidence you can offer of the truth of the gospel?

8. What is your church doing to ensure that future generations will always be able to remember these things Peter passed on to us? What is your family doing? What are you doing?

9. Imagine that you are faced with a person who says, "I'm just not sure that Jesus is the son of God." How will you respond?

PRAYER

Dear Father in heaven, hallowed be Your name. Give us the determination and diligence to teach others and reinforce the things they already know so that when we are gone from this world, others will be equipped to carry on Your mission.

ENEMIES WITHIN

2 Peter 2:1–22

Christians must be continually alert for false teaching.

The early church faced many threats. Some were from outside enemies, but the greatest danger came from within. The problem was false teachers. People who claimed to be students of Christ began emerging in various locations with new or distorted versions of the gospel. Some were chasing tangents, while others claimed to possess a new, superior knowledge of spiritual things. The same is true today. Ancient heresies never die, they are simply recycled after a hundred years or so. The church today is in no less danger from false teaching than it was in the first century.

This study deals with the problem of false teachers in the church. While we must be cautious about making an accusation about false teaching (a person may simply be uninformed or poorly trained as a teacher), we must also be vigilant about guarding the essential tenets of the Christian faith.

COMMENTARY

Second Peter has traditionally been broken into three chapters. This study focuses on the central chapter. Chapter 2 bounces back and forth between a description of the false teachers, their ideas, and the future they face as God prepares to judge them.

False Teachers and False Teaching, Part 1 (2 Pet. 2:1–3)

Chapter 1 ended by describing the authority of true prophets. God's Old Testament spokesmen accurately spoke and wrote

God's Word (1:19–21). Chapter 2 then begins by transitioning to the theme of false prophets. Its opening verse notes that the possibility of counterfeiting true teaching is not new, but nearly as old as the true teaching itself. In centuries past, **false prophets** (v. 1) mingled with the true. In the current period, just as Peter's readers had heard him and others proclaim the gospel of Jesus (1:1–11), false teachers would be approaching Christians and their gatherings, trying to cast doubt on God's truth (2:1).

WORDS FROM WESLEY

2 Peter 2:1

St. Peter wrote about the same time "to the strangers," the Christians, "scattered abroad through" all those spacious provinces of "Pontus, Galatia, Cappadocia, Asia" Minor, "and Bithynia." These, probably, were some of the most eminent Christians that were then in the world. Yet how exceeding far were even these from being "without spot and blemish!" And what grievous tares were here also growing up with the wheat! Some of them were "bringing in damnable heresies, even denying the Lord that bought them" (2 Pet. 2:1, &c.): And "many followed their pernicious ways;" of whom the apostle gives that terrible character: "They walk after the flesh," in "the lust of uncleanness, like brute beasts, made to be taken and destroyed. Spots they are, and blemishes, while they feast with you" (In the "feasts of charity," then celebrated throughout the whole church): "having eyes full of adultery, and that cannot cease from sin. These are wells without water, clouds that are carried with a tempest, for whom the mist of darkness is reserved for ever." And yet these very men were called Christians, and were even then in the bosom of the church! Nor does the apostle mention them as infesting any one particular church only; but as a general plague, which even then was dispersed far and wide among all the Christians to whom he wrote! (WJW, vol. 6, 259)

Their false teaching would include at least two components: (1) invented stories (v. 3) and (2) false doctrine (v. 1) based on those stories. Peter here implied a contrast to the true teaching that the apostles offered. In both evangelistic first contacts with pagans, as well as in follow-up ministry among new Christians, the apostles offered accurate accounts of all they had seen Jesus do and say (the material that we find written in the four gospels). People of all times love stories. But the counterfeiters could use the same method. They too came up with highly engaging stories, but their tales came straight out of their heads, without any basis in history. According to this false view of history, Jesus was neither the unique Son of God, nor a true human being, but instead merely a divine representative who only appeared to be human. Such stories, of course, denied **the sovereign Lord** (v. 1) who paid the price of salvation for all. False stories led to false doctrine, just as true stories had led people toward the truth.

As Peter straightforwardly said, **many will follow** the wrong **ways** (v. 2). That's bad enough, but Peter had not described the worst yet. Not only will some people go the wrong way, but their actions will confuse still other nonbelievers. Mixing up true teaching with false teaching, those influenced by false teachers will come up with new combinations. Skeptics then could lump all these "Jesus people" together. They then might unfairly mock or criticize true Christians based on what they've seen fake Christians do (v. 2). This confusion could hinder people from finding salvation in the true Jesus. Everyone potentially suffers.

Judgment on False Teachers, Part 1 (2 Pet. 2:3–10)

If pranksters today gets caught falsely reporting a fire to the fire department, they can be arrested and jailed. Why? They were just having a bit of fun, right? No. At minimum, they cost their city money (or took volunteer firefighters away from their routines). But even worse, if the false alarm hinders or prevents the squad from promptly reaching a true fire, then property or even lives can be lost. In this situation, those who present "false teaching" deserve punishment. But what about those who purposely prevent people from recognizing eternal spiritual truth? **Their condemnation has**

long been hanging over them, and their destruction has not been sleeping (v. 3). To support this conclusion, Peter offered several vivid historical examples of judgment.

Peter first alluded to disobedient **angels** (v. 4). He likely referred here to the apparent fall of Satan and a number of angels who followed the Evil One rather than remaining loyal to their Lord. Because Scripture offers no vivid description of this event, we are left to piece together this event from hints that appear throughout the Bible. Precisely what happened, we do not know. But Peter here clearly described God's ultimate judgment on the sinning angels—**hell . . . gloomy dungeons**, and something worse to come (v. 4).

WORDS FROM WESLEY

2 Peter 2:4

Cast them down to hell—The bottomless pit, a place of unknown misery; *delivered them*—Like condemned criminals to safe custody, as if bound with the strongest chains, in a dungeon *of darkness, to be reserved unto the judgment of the* great day: though still those chains do not hinder their often walking up and down, seeking whom may they devour. (ENNT)

Peter next turned his attention to the events surrounding the great **flood** (v. 5). Observing the early generations, God could not bear their continuing, flagrant sin, so He judged that generation with a flood that destroyed all life (see Gen. 6:5–7) except faithful Noah, his family, and the animals they gathered onto the ark (Gen. 7:1–5).

Last, Peter, skipping down a few generations but remaining in the early chapters of Genesis, portrayed the destruction of **Sodom and Gomorrah** (2 Pet. 2:6). As in the days before the flood, the residents of these two cities had fallen into sin so grievous (Gen. 18:20–21) that God could postpone judgment no longer. He burned those cities and their people **to ashes** (2 Pet. 2:6). At the same time, just as God had rescued Noah from the flood, God protected **righteous** Lot and his daughters from destruction (vv. 7–8).

Peter argued that the God who previously had acted decisively both to judge the ungodly and to preserve His people among them would again follow that same pattern. Those who knowingly **follow the corrupt desire of the sinful nature**, despising **authority** (v. 10) stand in special danger. While their destruction might not be immediate (at least in God's eyes, His action was "swift," v. 1), it was certain (v. 9).

WORDS FROM WESLEY

2 Peter 2:9

If darkness be occasioned by manifold and heavy and unexpected temptations, the best way of removing and preventing this is, to teach believers always to expect temptation, seeing they dwell in an evil world, among wicked, subtle, malicious spirits, and have an heart capable of all evil. Convince them that the whole work of sanctification is not, as they imagined, wrought at once; that when they first believe they are but as new-born babes, who are gradually to grow up, and may expect many storms before they come to the full stature of Christ. Above all, let them be instructed, when the storm is upon them, not to reason with the devil, but to pray; to pour out their souls before God, and show Him of their trouble. (WJW, vol. 6, 90–91)

When Peter was writing to the true church (1:1), why did he give so much attention to false teachers? He obviously wanted his readers to recognize the danger they faced and to resist it by remaining firmly in the truth. But also he wanted to assure them that they did not face the danger alone. God, who would judge those seeking to destroy the church, would also **rescue godly people from trials** (v. 9). Here Peter repeated reassuring thoughts from his first letter—those who endure hard times will grow strong through those difficult experiences (1 Pet. 4:12–19).

False Teachers and False Teaching, Part 2 (2 Pet. 2:10–19)

In the next paragraphs, Peter noted that ungodly actions accompanied the deceptive words of the false teachers. His charges against them continue to mount up.

They **are not afraid to slander celestial beings** (v. 10). These words might involve unfair treatment of earthly church leaders, but more likely refers to false accusations against angels or other divine creatures. What might this have involved? Again we can offer a theory. Perhaps they were foreshadowing subsequent second-century false teachers who announced that the God of the Old Testament was not the one true God, but a bumbling heavenly being who erred by placing the divine spark within material beings. In any case, the first-century false teachers, without hesitation, slandered heavenly beings they could not see or **understand** (v. 12). At the same time, God's angels (perhaps the target of the attack) refused to respond in kind. Perhaps even the angels had heard the words of Jesus; they "turned the other cheek" (Matt. 5:39).

Without shame, these sinful leaders **carouse[d] in broad daylight** (2 Pet. 2:13). Contemporary pagans often held orgies of food and sex, but at least did so behind closed doors. But the false Christians, perhaps glorying in sin "that grace might increase" (Rom. 6:1), felt that lawbreaking activity should be visible to all. (No wonder they brought "disrepute" on the true church; 2 Pet. 2:2.) Their feasting (v. 13) implies gluttony. Their **adultery** (v. 14) involves sexual sin. Their **greed** (v. 14) shows their self-centered focus on material possessions.

These people's false teaching (**empty, boastful words**, v. 18) gave them excuse for sinful behavior. Their sinful behavior (**appealing to the lustful desires of sinful human nature**, v. 18) required further lies as rationale. Words and deeds gave each other strength. These deluded people, enslaved by their sin, somehow felt they could offer **freedom** (v. 19) to those who joined them in slavery.

Peter not only offered literal descriptions of these sinners but also some choice analogies. Two millennia later, these pictures still combine to show a sad state. The false teachers were like **brute beasts** (v. 12) on their way to a meaningless death. Or they were like **blots and blemishes** (v. 13). A blotter (perhaps best described to new generations as an early form of paper towel) helped accident-prone people clean up their spills. One could never fully erase the stain. Unsightly blots often remained on important documents forever.

Peter also compared false teachers to **an accursed brood** (v. 14). Literally, the Greek behind this phrase reads, "children of the curse." Just as Jesus could describe Satan as the "father of lies" (John 8:44), meaning that he served as the ultimate source of all lies, so these people were children of the curse. Their actions had brought God's inescapable condemnation upon them.

They had **left the straight way** (2 Pet. 2:15). The wrong way they had chosen was the same one **Balaam** had selected centuries before. (Before the children of Israel entered the Promised Land, Balak, the King of Moab, wished to curse them. He convinced Balaam, one of his nation's prophets, to perform this act for him. Balaam tried several times, but God always hindered him, once even by enabling his **donkey** to speak to him, v. 16; see Num. 22–24.) It appears that Balaam, frustrated by God from cursing His people, devised another strategy. He tempted God's people away from the straight path by offering them the food and beautiful women of Moab.

These men are springs without water and mists driven by a storm (2 Pet. 2:17)—absolutely worthless.

WORDS FROM WESLEY
2 Peter 2:20–21

Those who so effectually know Christ, as by that knowledge to have escaped the pollutions of the world, may yet fall back into those pollutions, and perish everlastingly. . . .

That the knowledge of the way of righteousness, which they had attained, was an inward, experimental knowledge, is evident from that other expression—they had "escaped the pollutions of the world"; an expression parallel to that in the preceding chapter, verse 4: "Having escaped the corruption which is in the world." And in both chapters, this effect is ascribed to the same cause; termed in the first, "the knowledge of Him who hath called us to glory and virtue"; in the second, more explicitly, "the knowledge of the Lord and Saviour Jesus Christ."

And yet they lost that experimental knowledge of Christ and the way of righteousness; they fell back into the same pollutions they had escaped, and were "again entangled therein and overcome." They "turned from the holy commandment delivered to them," so that their "latter end was worse than their beginning."

Therefore, those who so effectually know Christ, as by that knowledge to have escaped the pollutions of the world, may yet fall back into those pollutions, and perish everlastingly. (WJW, vol. 10, 292–293)

Judgment on False Teachers, Part 2 (2 Pet. 2:20–22)

The previous paragraphs contain hints of judgment (vv. 12–13, 17, 19), but this chapter closes with a final summary of their destiny. It would have been better for these false teachers if they had never been born. They had once walked **the way of righteousness** (v. 21) but had rejected it. They had chosen for themselves, and all they could convince to follow them, to return to **the corruption of the world** (v. 20).

DISCUSSION

Peter warned that there would always be people who were eager to deceive and exploit followers of Christ by subtly leading them away from the truth of the gospel. He urged Christians to be on guard.

1. The early disciples were very concerned about false teachers leading new believers astray. What false teachers are present in our world today?

2. Name some of the false teachings you have heard. Which would you say is the most destructive?

3. Why do you think Peter identified "denying the sovereign Lord" (2 Pet. 2:1) as core of all false teaching?

4. What are other characteristics of false teachers? How can we identify them?

5. Why do you think false teachers are often effective in deceiving Christians?

6. Greed often characterizes false teachers today. Why would this be so common among false teachers? What is there about the church that would make it easy prey for such people?

7. Do you think you could recognize false teaching if you heard it? By what means would you identify it?

PRAYER

Almighty God, we cast ourselves before Your mercy, believing in Your willingness and ability to save us from the coming wrath. Give us the humility and confidence to escape this world through the knowledge of our Lord and Savior Jesus Christ.

CHRIST IS COMING!

2 Peter 3:1–18

The way to prepare for Christ's return is to live a holy life.

The seemingly long delay in Christ's coming has been a source of puzzlement and doubt for Christians since the first century. While Revelation insists that Jesus is coming "soon" and the apostle Paul seemed to expect that the return would occur during his lifetime, we find ourselves some two thousand years later still waiting and wondering when the event will take place. Is the Bible wrong? Did we misunderstand Jesus' teaching? Is He simply gone for good?

Peter wrote to a group of Christians who were asking similar questions. Like us, they were trying to balance the apparent teaching of Scripture with the fact that Christ's second coming seems to be taking much longer than anyone first thought. Peter's message? Leave the timing up to God, and keep yourself ready.

This study delves into an area of Christian teaching that seems always to cause speculation and wonder—the end times. While there are many things about the return of Christ that we cannot know, there are two things of which we are certain. The first is that Jesus will return, and the second is that we must be ready.

COMMENTARY

Second Peter's third chapter completes the biblical writings of this apostle. The first letter dealt with broad instructions for living as God's holy people. The second letter includes further general directions, but also specific information on several topics.

Peter's Purpose in Writing (2 Pet. 3:1–2)

Peter began the final chapter with an endearing phrase that appears two more times in this chapter, **Dear friends** (vv. 1, 14, 17). Did Peter know his life's end was coming? Perhaps from his Roman imprisonment, Peter pictured faces and names of people he loved, scattered across the churches of Asia Minor. In case there was any doubt, he wanted them to know how much he valued them.

As he reminisced, Peter not only recalled those among whom he had ministered, but also his ministry to them. **This is now my second letter to you** (v. 1). Peter wanted **to stimulate** them **to wholesome thinking** (v. 1). Peter, of course, felt equal concern for all components of his friends' being: bodies, spirits, souls, as well as minds. Perhaps he emphasized their thinking at this point to contrast it with the teaching of the imposters he had described in the previous chapter.

Peter then gathered a cloud of other witnesses around him. No false teacher could assert that Peter alone had offered the truth of God's salvation. Others had joined him in this task. Through their writings, **the holy prophets** (v. 2, likely here referring to Old Testament figures, although the wording does not rule out New Testament preacher-prophets) contributed their supporting testimony. Jesus, the **Lord and Savior** had borne witness to himself. Through a host of **apostles** (including Paul, see vv. 15–16), Peter's readers had heard Jesus' teaching (v. 2).

Before moving into the new content with which Peter finished the book, he wanted one more time to remind readers of the unified authority that stood behind his writing. What they read in his letter about Christ's return and the end of the world, they could trust, no matter what else they might hear.

Christ Will Return, Despite the Scoffers (2 Pet. 3:3–10)

You have heard the old proverb "Forewarned is forearmed." Evidently, Peter recognized this truth centuries ago. He warned the Christians that while they waited to see Jesus again, some among them might begin to doubt.

In the earliest days of the church, Jesus' followers had interpreted His words to mean that He would return within a few years. As the decades passed, Peter and others began to realize that they might have misunderstood; perhaps it might yet be awhile. Peter could not say *when* Jesus would descend from heaven, but he never doubted that Jesus would. But Peter sensed that, as time went on, some in the church would begin to question, **"Where is this 'coming'** Jesus **promised? Ever since our fathers died, everything goes on as it has since the beginning of creation"** (v. 4).

From our perspective, we can easily confirm the truth of Peter's prediction. Who among us has not heard such scoffing? Perhaps we can admit that even we have faced days when we wondered, "When will Christ come and restore His kingdom? Why not now?"

For both the **scoffers (following their own evil desires**, v. 3) and for us, with occasional honest doubt, Peter offered several counterarguments. How can we know that Christ still will return?

First, we can see valid evidence in the history of God's creation of, and interaction with, the world. Even in their scoffing, the skeptics began to refute their own doubts. As soon as they mentioned the **beginning of creation** (v. 4), they should remember the identity and character of the loving, powerful Creator. Could this world have come into being on its own? Of course not. Would He who spoke the world into existence abandon His handiwork? Never! He who has remained an active participant in its history would not let His creation fade out of existence.

No, when it's time for earth's grand finale, God himself will engineer its final moments. Just as God determined the date for earth's first act to end, when He flooded its territory (v. 6, note also 2:5), God will pull the final curtain on His cosmic drama. With the same voice (see Peter's use of **word** in 3:5, 7) that called the earth into being, with the same hands that created the first human being, God will judge the world and its **ungodly** inhabitants (v. 7).

How can we know that, no matter how long it takes, Christ will return? First, history offers its confirmation. If that's not enough, the Old Testament speaks its word too. **With the Lord a day is like a thousand years, and a thousand years are like a day** (v. 8). Perhaps Peter stretched his imagination as far as it would go, dreaming that it might be as long as a thousand years before the end of the world. Even so, from God's perspective that would be no more than a mere twenty-four hours. No matter who decides that God is **slow** (v. 9), He is acting in His own good time. Jesus may have said that He would return *quickly*, but for human beings and for God, that word contains two quite different meanings. God will keep His **promise**. Old Testament Scripture confirms that.

WORDS FROM WESLEY

2 Peter 3:8

You know a day, an hour, a moment, with God, is as a thousand years. He cannot be straitened for time, wherein to work whatever remains to be done in your soul. And God's time is always the best time. (WJW, vol. 6, 40)

Similarly, the very character of God himself guarantees that He will not let us down. If the Lord delays His return, no one should think He has forgotten us. No one should worry that He has turned His back. God may be purposely postponing the end. Why? To give still more people time to believe and find salvation (v. 9; see also

v. 15). In God's grace, He holds hope that **everyone** (v. 9), perhaps even some **ungodly . . . scoffers** (vv. 7, 3), might again come to faith. Just as God warned Abraham and Lot of Sodom and Gomorrah's imminent destruction so Lot and his family could escape (Gen. 18:20; 19:13), so God warns everyone of the coming universal destruction, so that any who believe and **come to repentance** may not **perish**, but have everlasting life (2 Pet. 3:9; see John 3:16).

WORDS FROM WESLEY

2 Peter 3:9

If you ask, "Why then are not all men saved?" the whole law and the testimony answer. First, Not because of any decree of God; not because it is His pleasure they should die; for, "As I live, saith the Lord God," "I have no pleasure in the death of him that dieth" (Ezek. 18:3, 32). Whatever be the cause of their perishing, it cannot be His will, if the oracles of God are true; for they declare, "He is not willing that any should perish, but that all should come to repentance" (2 Pet. 3:9). (WJW, vol. 7, 381)

The second half of 2 Peter 3:10 pictures the overwhelming explosion that will destroy the earth. Should we take these words literally? Or do they merely offer the perfect picture of God's final fireworks? Some interpret these words as a first-century description of the ultimate nuclear disaster. Perhaps some overwhelming world war will be the tool God uses to wrap up things here. Even if that happens, we need not worry that God will be caught off guard. He alone sets the expiration date for our planet.

Peter did not finish this discussion without supporting the truth of Christ's return with one more type of evidence. Already he has shown how Old Testament history, Old Testament testimony, and the character of God the Father all stand behind the trustworthiness of God's promise for the future. What evidence is left? The words of Jesus himself. In one of the epistles' clearest quotations of

Jesus, Peter stated words that perhaps seared into his mind from their first utterance: **the day of the Lord will come like a thief** (v. 10, paraphrasing Luke 12:39–40; see also 1 Thess. 5:2).

What was Peter's logic behind this quotation? He was saying, in effect, "Nobody should really be surprised that Jesus has not yet returned. After all, that's just how He said it would be." Peter stated that no one could know when Jesus would return. Despite the universal confusion about the timing, despite even our occasional doubts about His coming at all, Jesus will return. We can bank on that.

While Waiting for God, Live Like God (2 Pet. 3:11–14)

If you ever need an example of a dramatic rhetorical question, remember Peter's words from 3:11: **Since everything will be destroyed in this way, what kind of people ought you to be?** Jesus, Paul, and Peter all said, in effect. "Since you know the thief is coming, sooner or later, what precautions ought you to be taking?" Or, closer to reality, "Since you know the world, all its glory, and all the possessions you cherish so much will all be taken from you— **the heavens** will be destroyed **by fire, and the** earth's **elements will melt in the heat** (v. 12)—what should be your priorities?"

WORDS FROM WESLEY

2 Peter 3:12

Hastening on—As it were, by your earnest desires and fervent prayers, *the coming of the day of God*—Many myriads of days He grants to men; one, the last, is the day of God himself. (ENNT)

Fortunately, Peter's question turns out not to be so rhetorical. In verses 11 and 14, he answered it himself: **You ought to live holy and godly lives. . . . Make every effort to be found spotless, blameless and at peace with him**. As Peter began his first epistle with God's command to be holy as He is holy (1 Pet. 1:16), he finished his second letter on the same note. Holiness of course contains two complementary elements: being set apart and being morally clean. Peter's collection of synonyms support that twofold definition.

Be godly—be devoted completely to God; follow His ways.

Be spotless and blameless—let none of the false teachers' "blots and blemishes" (2 Pet. 2:13) stain your life. Both their incorrect thoughts and inappropriate actions keep them from knowing and following God. Instead, Peter must have been saying, "Believe the truth. Live in accordance with God's plan."

Live **at peace with** God (3:14). Those who truly know Him, those who walk in His ways, experience an open relation of peace with Him, a peace that nothing can take away (John 14:27). No matter what happens in this life, they know that, in accordance **with his promise**, God will welcome His people into **a new heaven and a new earth** He is planning (2 Pet. 3:13).

Peter's Final Remarks (2 Pet. 3:15–18)

Peter closed his letter with one comparison and one contrast. The comparison? What Peter had written in this letter bears overwhelming similarity to what Paul had previously written (v. 15). Perhaps Peter here alluded to the scriptural principle: "Where two witnesses agree, their testimony is trustworthy." (See Deut. 19:15; Matt. 18:16.)

While dealing with the fact that Paul's teaching agreed with his own, Peter offered an aside comment that has comforted Bible scholars throughout the centuries. If even Peter, a central apostle, did not **understand** everything that Paul had written (2 Pet. 3:16), then none of us need to feel any shame when we can't quite figure out all of Paul's meaning. At the same time, Peter offered the greatest compliment to his colleague; he grouped Paul's writings with **the other Scriptures** (v. 16). Here we see the first hint that writings later collected as the New Testament could be placed on the same high level as the valued texts of Moses, Samuel, and the prophets.

After comparing his writings with Paul's, Peter contrasted his knowledge of the truth with the false teachers who think they offer accurate words, but in reality teach **error** (v. 17). Peter recognized the unfortunate fact that false teaching often does include much truth. He saw that people could even **distort** the meaning of inspired Scripture, resulting in **their own destruction** (v. 16) and the misdirection of their gullible followers. Peter again reminded his readers to stay close to what he had taught them, to stay close to orthodox teaching about Christ. If they did so, their **position** would remain **secure** (v. 17).

Yet at the same time, believers could not rest too securely in their present state. If they spiritually stagnated, they might regress and thus become more vulnerable to temptation. Instead, they should continue **to grow in the grace** (their relationship with Jesus) **and knowledge** (their awareness of the truth) **of our Lord and Savior Jesus Christ** (v. 18). He is the unshakable center of life. **To him be glory both now and forever! Amen** (v. 18).

WORDS FROM WESLEY

2 Peter 3:18

I use this expression, means of grace, because I know none better; and because it has been generally used in the Christian church for many ages—in particular by our own church, which directs us to bless God both for the means of grace, and hope of glory; and teaches us, that a sacrament is "an outward sign of inward grace, and a means whereby we receive the same."

The chief of these means are prayer, whether in secret or with the great congregation; searching the Scriptures (which implies reading, hearing, and meditating thereon); and receiving the Lord's Supper, eating bread and drinking wine in remembrance of Him: And these we believe to be ordained of God, as the ordinary channels of conveying His grace to the souls of men. (WJW, vol. 5, 187–188)

DISCUSSION

The Christian hope is built on the promise that Christ will return and decisively establish His new creation. Peter urged his readers to prepare their lives for Christ's return.

1. What do you think Peter meant by "wholesome thinking" (2 Pet. 3:1)? What would be unwholesome thinking?

2. In what way can we stimulate wholesome thinking in each other? What are the things we might do that provoke unwholesome thoughts in others?

3. In Peter's day, some people scoffed at the idea that Jesus would return to the earth. Have you encountered scoffing or other criticism at the claims of Christ? What form did it take? How did you respond?

4. One reason people found it hard to accept the idea that Jesus would return was that His coming seemed to have been delayed for a long time. How does the gap in time between Jesus' ascension and His return affect your faith?

5. Have you ever wondered why God seems to be taking so long to fulfill His promises?

6. Peter offered one reason for God's delay: He is eager to see more people have eternal life. On a scale from one to ten, how would you rate your church's passion for evangelism?

7. If we really believed that Jesus could return at any moment, how might we change the way we live? The way we conduct ourselves as a church?

PRAYER

Dear Lord, help us to pray with the apostle John, "Come, Lord Jesus." And may the grace of the Lord Jesus Christ be with God's people.

CONTENDING FOR THE FAITH

Jude 1–25

Every Christian is responsible to become more mature in the faith.

From parents to business managers, nearly everyone who deals with people has heard, "That's not my job." Whether because we feel incompetent to take on the challenge or simply don't want to take on new work, most of us are good at narrowly defining our responsibilities at work or at home—even at church.

So whose responsibility is it to ensure that that church works the way it should? In particular, who is responsible to ensure that the truth is taught, false ideas do not infiltrate the church and lead others astray, and Christians become mature in their faith? Is it pastors? District superintendents? College professors? And who is responsible for your maturity in Christ?

You are, according to Jude. This study levels a clear challenge to every member of the church to "contend for the faith that was once for all entrusted to the saints" (Jude 3). The spiritual integrity and maturity of the church is not a matter for professionals alone; it is our responsibility to see that the truth is taught and that the church grows strong and healthy.

COMMENTARY

The little book of Jude is remarkable in several ways. It is only one chapter long, twenty-five verses. Because Jude refers to an episode recorded only in the Assumption of Moses (from a group of extra-biblical writings called the Pseudepigrapha) and quotes the apocryphal book of 1 Enoch, Jude was hotly disputed when final decisions were being made on the New Testament canon. Because Jude, the half-brother of Jesus, was regarded as the book's author, the church decided it belongs in the New Testament.

Jude wrote to a people facing the danger of false teachers who had infiltrated the churches. Any believers who listened to them were in danger of being turned from the faith. Jude wrote with an urgency born out of a sense of crisis; Jude knew he dare not lose any time urging and instructing the faithful, or they, too, could be deceived by plausible-sounding arguments.

Greeting (Jude 1–2)

Jude identified himself as **a servant of Jesus Christ and a brother of James** (v. 1). This was neither of the Jameses of Jesus' band of disciples; neither had a brother named Jude (or Judah, its Hebrew form). But James who wrote the book of James did have a brother named Jude. This James was a half-brother of Jesus, so it follows that Jude was also. James was the leading figure in the Jewish church in Jerusalem and Judea until he was martyred in A.D. 62. We know little of Jude's leadership roles in the church; he may have mentioned his relationship with his more prominent brother to lend credibility to his message for any readers or hearers who did not know him.

To those who have been called (v. 1), with no specific city or people named, places Jude among the letters called the General Epistles. Jude may have sent one original letter that circulated to various churches or several copies to several churches. It is possible in cases like this that each church, as it received the letter, made a copy, then sent it on to another church.

WORDS FROM WESLEY

Jude 1

Jude, a servant of Jesus Christ—The highest glory which any, either angel or man, can aspire to. The word *servant*, under the old covenant, was adapted to the spirit of fear and bondage that clave to that dispensation. But when the time appointed of the Father was come, for the sending of His Son to redeem them that were under the law, the word *servant* (used by the apostles concerning themselves and all the children of God) signified one that having the spirit of adoption is *made free* by the Son of God. His being a *servant* is the fruit and perfection of his being a son. And whenever the throne of God and of the Lamb shall be in the New Jerusalem, then will it be indeed that *his servants shall serve him*, Rev. 22. (ENNT)

Change of Subject (Jude 3–4)

Jude indicated that he had intended to write for some time, being **very eager to write to you about the salvation we share** (v. 3). But disturbing news had come to him, and the need to write became urgent, because of a serious threat to the spiritual health of the believers. He had to urge them **to contend for the faith** (v. 3) in this crisis atmosphere.

What was the crisis that changed Jude's agenda in writing? It was false teaching brought in by **certain men**. Jude identified this false teaching as turning **the grace of our God into a license for immorality** (v. 4). This heresy, already stressing the church by the middle of the first century, came later to be known as Gnosticism.

Gnosticism teaches that since we can do nothing to earn our salvation, and since God's forgiveness of our sins is based entirely on His grace, then what we do—even after our salvation—makes no difference, whether we do good or evil. This heresy is made more seductive by the assertion that it is a secret, higher knowledge, hidden from the common Christian, available only to those with superior spiritual sensibilities. This in itself is a way of denying **Jesus Christ** (v. 4), because it cheapens the seriousness of

His atonement for our sins on the cross. But it also denies that the Christian is called to follow after Christ in our attitudes and actions, in the development of our character in godliness.

Description of False Teachers (Jude 5–16)

Jude began his argument against these early Gnostics who had managed to make their way into the fellowship of believers, by reminding his readers of three examples from the Old Testament, examples they knew very well. God delivered all Israel from **Egypt**, but **those who did not believe** (v. 5) perished in the wilderness because of their unbelief, in spite of what they had experienced.

In Jude's second example (v. 6), he probably was referring to Genesis 6:1–4, since 1 Enoch comments on that passage, and in verse 14 Jude quotes 1 Enoch 1:9. The angels Jude referred to here also refused to follow God and lost their first estate.

Jude's final example is **Sodom and Gomorrah** (Jude 7), destroyed by God because of the people's unbelief and gross sexual transgression, among other sins. All of these examples involved deliberate and flagrant sexual sin, in the estimation of first-century commentators, both Christian and Jewish. Jude chose them because the false teachers he argued against in this epistle lived and taught that sexual (along with other) immorality does not matter.

Jude next began to characterize the corrupt nature of these false teachers in vivid language, while continuing to refer to similar behavior in the past, from episodes with which his readers would have been familiar. In verse 8, Jude began by calling them **dreamers**. He probably had in mind the means by which these false teachers received their so-called "new revelations," which would have included claiming to receive some of them in dreams. But Jude also meant this as a dismissal of these men and their supposed dreams; both were worthless—worse still, they were dangerous.

Because they did not understand—in spite of their claims to being the knowing ones—these false teachers committed serious transgressions, and taught others to do the same. They polluted **their own bodies** (v. 8). In all eras, sexual immorality cancels one's ability to treat the body as the temple of God, and lessens the capacity to present it to one's spouse as the delightful gift God intended it to be.

They **reject authority** (v. 8), literally, "lordship," that is, the lordship of Christ. Their teaching is destructive of persons, and of relationships with God and with fellow humans. That alone is sufficient evidence that these false teachers (then and now) are rejecting Christ's lordship.

They **slander celestial beings** (v. 8), literally, "they blaspheme glories." Jude's point here is that these false teachers were so ignorant of the heavenly realities that they did not hesitate to speak lightly, disrespectfully, even slanderously, of glorious personages in the heavenlies about whom they knew absolutely nothing.

By contrast, Jude said, **Michael** the **archangel**—whom we may suppose knows nearly everything about the orders of heavenly beings—did not consider it proper to "speak revilingly" against **the devil** himself (v. 9). If the archangel is content with **"The Lord rebuke you!"** then we humans should be circumspect in our speech regarding people we don't know much about. Hubris is not the mark of a great teacher; rather, it is a danger signal.

These false teachers **speak abusively against whatever they do not understand** (v. 10). Jude continued to use the same Greek word here—*blaspheme*, revile. What they do know, they **understand by instinct, like unreasoning animals** (v. 10), that is, they do not have to think about it. Not thinking, acting like the unreasoning lower animal creation, is another oblique reference to promiscuous sexual behavior and other destructive practices.

Jude now referenced briefly three other disobedient persons from the pages of the Old Testament: **Cain** and **Korah** (v. 11).

Balaam (v. 11) is not censured for rebellion against God in the chapters from Numbers where his story is told. But a tradition survived that he taught Balak, King of Moab, how to snare the Israelites in sexual sin at Baal-Peor.

In verses 12–13, Jude stitched together an extraordinary string of startlingly vivid metaphors, six in all. **Love feasts** in the early church were among the most sacred (as well as joyous) symbolic acts of the believers. These false teachers were **blemishes** at these love feasts, because they brought their immoral teachings and actions into these most sacred occasions.

Jude's other five metaphors seem to emphasize the futility of these men and their empty teaching, which brings all its adherents to destruction in the end. **Shepherds who feed only themselves** (v. 12) do not benefit the sheep, but rather destroy them. (**Shepherds** is implied, though with good reason; the word does not occur in the Greek text, which is why NASB does not have it.) **Clouds without rain** are fraudulent, and benefit no one. **Autumn trees** should be laden; these not only are **without fruit**, but are **uprooted** and, therefore, **twice dead** (v. 12).

Two more symbols of futility round out this gallery of vivid word pictures. **Wild waves of the sea** (v. 13) toss continuously in a never-ending cycle, yet the shoreline never retreats. The foam is their **shame**; its lightweight, vain, temporary character describes perfectly the nothingness that is these men's teaching. Finally, real **stars** shine brightly, reliably, permanently. But these men are **wandering stars**, or meteors, flashing brilliantly across the horizon for a moment, then disappearing into **blackest darkness . . . forever** (v. 13).

Jude's fourfold repetition of one word, **ungodly**, in verse 15, is almost unique in the Bible. It underscores his condemnation of these disturbers of the peace of the Christian assemblies they had wormed their way into. It also leads into verse 16 with its five-count indictment of their conduct in the churches. Such conduct is more than disruptive and destructive. It is ungodly, and this indictment would form the basis of God's judgment upon them when it fell, as it was sure to do.

Exhortation to Faithfulness (Jude 17–23)

Following up on his scathing indictment, Jude was content with the briefest of warm reminders to all those he was confident would take his warnings to heart. He began, **But, dear friends, remember** (v. 17). They would be safeguarded by his current warning delivered by this letter, and by recalling that **the apostles** already had forewarned them that such **scoffers** would appear **in the last times** (v. 18). Anxiety was not warranted; forewarned is forearmed, and Christ was their strength.

WORDS FROM WESLEY

Jude 20

But ye, beloved—Not separating, but *building yourselves up in your most holy faith*—Than which none can be more holy in itself, or more conducive to the most refined and exalted holiness: *praying through the Holy Spirit*—Who alone is able to build you up, as he alone laid the foundation. (ENNT)

Verses 20–21 contain an excellent summary of the personal disciplines for a healthy life in the Christian faith: **build yourselves up . . . pray in the Holy Spirit . . . keep yourselves in God's love . . . wait for the mercy of our Lord Jesus Christ**. The specific ways in which a believer does these things may be somewhat different from era to era, from believer to believer. But if these attitudes and goals inform our speech and actions, we will not be susceptible to the dangers of false teachings against which Jude so vigorously warned.

WORDS FROM WESLEY

Jude 21

I believe, very easily: St. Jude's exhortation, "Keep yourselves in the love of God," certainly implies that something is to be done on our part, in order to its continuance. And is not this agreeable to that declaration of our Lord, concerning this and every gift of God? "Unto him that hath shall be given, and he shall have more abundance: But from him that hath not"—that is, uses it not, improves it not—"shall be taken away even that which he hath" (Luke 8:18). (WJW, vol. 7, 41)

In that strength and assurance, Jude was confident, the believer may reach out to others without endangering him- or herself. To those who are wavering between the truth and the seductions of the false teachers, **be merciful** (v. 22). Do not be afraid even to **snatch others from the fire** (v. 23) those who already had succumbed to the false logic of the deceivers. Do not be overconfident, however. **Mixed with fear** (v. 23) reflects the knowledge that if we rely on our own strength rather than Christ's, we will rescue no one, but be in great danger of losing ourselves.

Sublime Benediction (Jude 24–25)

Eminently suitable is Jude's benedictory doxology: **To him who is able to keep you from falling** (v. 24). Great as was the danger from the false teachers, Jesus' power was and is infinitely greater. Jude's first readers (and us today) need not to fear; He is able to and will **present you before his glorious presence without fault and with great joy**. To the sublime climax of this majestic doxology (v. 25), we may only bow our heads and say, "Even so, come, Lord Jesus!"

DISCUSSION

The letter of Jude offers not only a strong warning not to be led astray by false teachers but an even stronger promise that God is able to keep us from falling away from Him. Jude urged believers to remain in God's love.

1. Like Peter, Jude was very concerned about false teachers. How did he characterize them?

2. One common characteristic of false teachers is that they are sexually immoral. Which do you think comes first, a willingness to accept false ideas about the faith or the desire for sexual sin?

3. Jude taught that the core of false teaching is to "deny Jesus Christ our only Sovereign and Lord" (Jude 4). What evidence do you see in today's church that belief in Jesus Christ as the Son of God is under attack?

4. How can we avoid being deceived by false teachers?

5. What are some things we might do to ensure that our friends or family members are not taken in by such teachers?

6. Can you think of any questionable statements you have heard from religious teachers or read in books? How did you identify them? What told you they were false?

7. How well does your church or small group identify correct versus incorrect statements about the faith?

8. Many Christians experience doubts about the faith. How can we best encourage them?

PRAYER

Most majestic and almighty God, please keep us from falling, and bring us soon into Your glorious presence so that our joy may be complete. Until then, help us to seek justice, love mercy, and walk humbly in Your sight.

WORDS FROM WESLEY WORKS CITED

ENNT: *Explanatory Notes upon the New Testament,* by John Wesley, M.A. Fourth American Edition. New York: J. Soule and T. Mason, for the Methodist Episcopal Church in the United States, 1818.

PW: *The Poetical Works of John and Charles Wesley.* Edited by D. D. G. Osborn. 13 vols. London: Wesleyan-Methodist Conference Office, 1868.

WJW: *The Works of John Wesley.* Third Edition, Complete and Unabridged. 14 vols. London: Wesleyan Methodist Book Room, 1872.

OTHER BOOKS IN THE
WESLEY BIBLE STUDIES SERIES

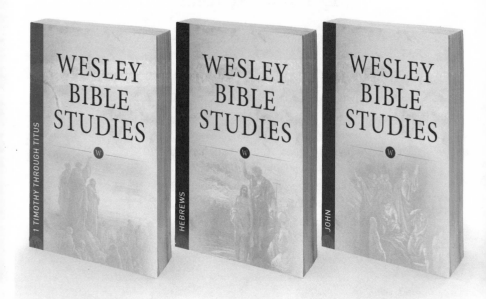